FRIDAYS WITH FREDDIE

ONE MAN'S VICTORY OVER LIFE'S ADVERSITIES AND THE PRINCIPLES HE PASSED ON TO A COMPLETE STRANGER

CHRISTOPHER BLAIRE

TABLE OF CONTENTS

PART I

TWO PROFILES

FREDDIE'S STORY

Chapter One

FORCED TO GROW UP

> You never know how strong you are until being strong is the only choice you have.
>
> ~ *Bob Marley*

War has a certain smell. A certain sound. You can taste it. I can't describe it. Even if I could, you wouldn't be able to understand it any more than a woman could describe to a man the anguish of giving birth. There is nothing to compare it to.

Strange thing about a jungle. Everything in it, including the jungle itself wants to kill you. Sounds take on extraordinary meanings in your imagination. A snap of a twig, a squeal or creak that seems out of the ordinary creates a million scenarios in your mind. In the absolute darkness nothing is more disturbing than silence and nothing more dangerous. When the jungle is quiet you know nothing and expect everything – and it's all bad. At least when the bullets are flying there is no more haunting fear of expectations. You are engaged, alive. Your life takes on a new kind of purpose. You have meaning.

I couldn't believe I was here. Just a few months ago I was watching sunsets and sunrises sipping on Mai Tais with the love of my life on the majestic sands of Honolulu, Hawaii. Now I was dodging bullets and mosquitoes in the jungles of Vietnam.

How had all this happened to me?

My Beginnings

I was born Fredrick Clemett in 1947 on September 15 to Leslie Clemett and Yojin Chang at Adelphi hospital in Brooklyn New York. My father was of Welsh and German descent and a career military man through and through. He met my mother in Shanghai during World War II.

Our family bounced around during my childhood due to my father's career in the military – Brooklyn, Queens, Thailand, Okinawa Japan, and finally we landed in Honolulu a few months before my eighteenth birthday. Since we were always moving around, I became an expert at making friends quickly, so I could stay at their homes and have a place to hide when the insanity erupted in my house. It wasn't uncommon for me to spend a few nights a week and all of my time during the day away from my house where my father would terrorize me, my mother and brother.

Growing up, I had an older brother nineteen months my senior named Lloyd. For whatever reason, my father hated my brother. The beatings started early. One of my youngest memories as a child was my father smashing my brother's face on the kitchen table breaking his nose. I was probably five years old at the time. Those events happened almost daily in our household.

My father would drink whiskey the moment he stepped home from work and we never knew if Dr. Jekyll or Mr. Hyde was going to show up. It was mostly the bad guy Mr. Hyde. Whenever he would fly off into a rage, even at a very young age, my brother Lloyd would step in front of me to absorb the abuse. When I wasn't hiding at a friend's house, I would be hiding in my safe spot in my closet under a pile of clothes where my father couldn't find me even if he tried.

Lloyd wasn't so lucky. We were living in Okinawa and after so many years of abuse, as soon as my brother turned eighteen, my father gave him a one-way plane ticket, $50 and told him, "Here's 50 bucks. It's the first and last money you'll ever get from me. Get out of my house and never come back." That's the kind of monster my father was. Now that my brother was out of the house, I knew it was only a matter of time before my father would turn his wrath on me. Luckily, he got transferred not too long after kicking Lloyd out of the house, and we moved to Honolulu.

I couldn't have been more excited to get out of that tiny apartment in Japan and experience the beauty and new life that Hawaii had to offer. We had a family friend who moved there a year prior, and he had a son around my age. I took to Honolulu with all the zeal of someone just released from prison. I was finally free to be me and experience all the life I could pack into Hawaii.

The year was 1966 and I was living the life, eighteen years old and not a care in the world. I was crashing at my friend's house most days during the week, trying to avoid the nightmare of my family life at home with my father. I got a job at the local fish market so I would have some spending money as we tore up the town.

Then it happened...

I never believed in love at first sight, but I now know it's as real as rain. It was a mystical summer night in Honolulu. A gentle breeze blew off the ocean as the tempo of Polynesian drums lured me closer to the stage of the resort where hula dancers moved in perfect harmony with the music. As I approached the stage, I couldn't take my eyes off one of the girls. I don't know what it was; it seemed like an amber glowing aura surrounded her. She looked over at me in mid dance and our eyes locked for what seemed an eternity. She knew. I knew.

Her name was Leilani and she was the most beautiful woman I'd ever met both on the inside and outside. We were young kids in the prime of our lives exploring love and the magnificence that was Hawaii. All the pain and horror of my childhood would melt away as I gazed into her eyes while we held hands and walked along the golden beaches of Honolulu.

I was on a permanent honeymoon. I was getting a lot of overtime at the local fish market slinging tuna all day. The work was disgusting, but I did what I had to do preparing for my future with my Hawaiian Princess.

Leilani was from an old- fashioned traditional Hawaiian family that had been living on the island for hundreds of years. They immediately welcomed me with open arms. There is an enduring tradition in the Hawaiian culture where the family extends wide and far, welcoming and embracing others into their circle of love. They call it *ohana*. I finally found what I had been looking for: a loving family who accepted me unconditionally. My future seemed bright like the glow in Leilani's eyes. But my paradise on earth was soon to come crashing down around me.

The Vietnam War was raging in Southeast Asia and it was only a matter of time before my number was up and I would get drafted. One rare Saturday morning when I was actually home, my father sat me down at the kitchen table with a pen in his hand and shoved a biblical-sized contract in front of me.

"What's this?" I questioned as I halfheartedly leafed through the document.

"Don't worry about it. Go to the last page and sign it," my father commanded. Still unaware of what was in front of me, I flipped over the contract and peeled back the last page and perused some of the paragraphs. It was an agreement for me to enlist in the United States Navy.

"What the heck is this? The Navy?" I asked.

"Yeah, you're not going to the jungles of Vietnam to get your head blown off. You're going into the Navy where you'll be safe on the ocean and not have to worry about getting drafted into the Army or the Marines," my father said.

"But Dad, I want to go to college and build my life with Leilani here in Hawaii. That's what I've been planning for the past nine months," I retorted.

"You're too stupid to get into college and that girl of yours, if she really loves you, will wait for you to get back from serving your country. Now sign on the dotted line!" he demanded with all the force of a drill sergeant. I was only eighteen, and even though my father was a heartless monster, I still knew he had much more life experience than I did, and his powers of persuasion were starting to wear me down.

He calmed down a bit and reasoned with me. "This is a better way for you, Freddie. You'll see the world, become a man, gain respect and you can save a lot more money for your life with Leilani by doing a tour in the Navy than you ever could working that horrible job for the next two years. What are you going to do? Work at the fish market while you go to school and come home every night to your new bride reeking of old tuna fish?

"Besides, it's only two years. It'll fly by. Then then you can come back to Hawaii and start your life with Leilani in the proper manner – as a veteran of the United States Navy. No more fish market. You can write your own ticket. On top of all that, you will get the GI Bill which will pay for your college. It's the best bet for you now and for your future life, Freddie."

His logic was starting to forge cracks in the walls of resistance in my mind. "He's right," I silently started to convince myself. "This fish market business is kind of disgusting and can I really do it for the next four years to pay my way through college?" As much as I hated my father for what he had done to my brother and mother, I still held on to that childish instinct of looking up to him. He was after all my father. Besides, two years would fly by. I could return to Hawaii, marry Leilani in the proper fashion with a wedding fit for a Hawaiian princess and I would have the G.I. Bill, so I wouldn't have to worry about paying for college.

My father was as much a salesman as he was a barbarian, and he knew how to get me to do what he wanted.

"Trust me, Freddie; she'll wait for you. You'll come back a man she can respect and admire, and the Navy will give that to you I promise. More importantly, you won't be going to that cesspool,

Vietnam," he told me with all the suaveness of a late-night talk show host.

He pushed the pen across the table and smiled, "Trust me – just sign on the dotted line."

I had rarely seen my father smile, let alone that sort of bizarre sadistic smile – if you can call it that. I can still see it in my mind today. His persistence and charm somehow got my hand to magically sign my name on the dotted line. I didn't bother to read the contract. I assumed my father had read it already and everything was square business.

Note to self: any time you sign a contract, read the whole document...especially the fine print!

What my father had failed to tell me, either through careless omission or heartless intent, was that my term in the Navy was for four years not two. By the time I found out, it was too late. I was somewhere in the middle of nowhere on the USS Ticonderoga floating in the Pacific Ocean.

The night before my ship sailed off, I brought Leilani to our favorite restaurant for the best and worst night of my life. Leilani took the news of my enlistment just as I thought she would. She cried all night as we walked along the same beach we had done a thousand times before. We promised we would stay faithful and wait for each other until I returned.

Unfortunately, Uncle Sam had other plans for my life.

Chapter Two

A RUDE AWAKENING

> Nothing in life is so exhilarating as to be shot at without result.
>
> ~ *Winston Churchill*

The Navy shipped me off to San Diego to spend four months in Naval boot camp and assigned me to the USS Ticonderoga CVA14 World War II class aircraft carrier. I was a yeoman working as a clerk managing work assignments for the ship's maintenance. It was my first job since the fish market, and for the first time in my life, my father was actually right about something. The uniforms, the discipline, the responsibility – I was a new man. Leilani would respect me even more when I got back because for the first time in my life I was starting to respect myself.

Quickly rising through the ranks to the level of E-4 and becoming a Boatswain mate, I was essentially running the ship. Over sixty people reported to me, and I was responsible for coordinating supplies for the ship like fuel, food, and bombs. It was a big job for anyone, let alone a nineteen year old kid. Traveling around the world on Uncle Sam's dime, our ship visited exotic ports of call. I became very familiar with the Philippines, Hong Kong, Thailand, Malaysia – just to name a few.

My future couldn't have looked brighter.

Leilani and I stayed as close as possible, given the circumstances, writing each other every chance we got. In spite of the distance, our love grew stronger. Absence truly makes the heart grow fonder...at least up to a certain point.

Every Monday was mail call, my favorite day of the week because I would get letters the size of small novels from Leilani. I stood in line, along with all the soldiers on the ship, waiting to hear my name shouted from the sergeant standing on a podium handing out the mail. When I heard my name called, I would run to the front of the line and eagerly snatch the mail out of his hand. I couldn't wait to open Leilani's letters and smell her perfume sprinkled across her notes. We would write to each other in detail about our plans to get married and raise our family on the island, remembering the times we strolled the shores of Honolulu and the cookouts every Saturday with her *ohana*. She was going to become a teacher, and I was going to attend college and get a job in government.

As I was walking away from the sergeant, mail in hand, heading back to my barracks, the sergeant screamed my name, "Hey Clemett, you forgot something!" He was waving another piece of mail in the air. I rushed back with the same enthusiasm, hoping Leilani had sent me another letter the Navy had forgotten to hand me.

I couldn't have been more wrong or more horrified.

The front of the letter had all the sterile markings of a government document: black and white and cold as ice. I could feel the "badness" of what was inside the letter seeping into my palms before I opened it. I didn't know what it was for, but I knew it couldn't be good. As I peeled open the envelope the letter fell out onto the floor. Another bad omen. The letter said I was to report to Camp Pendleton in San Diego in the next ten days for further "instructions."

My father's brilliant scheme to outwit Uncle Sam had backfired. I was officially to become part of the United States Marine

Corp Force Reconnaissance Division, get trained to navigate and drive swift boats and LCM8s, otherwise officially known as landing craft mechanized boats, designed exclusively to carry Marines up and down the Mekong Delta in the narrow rivers of Vietnam.

After two years on the naval carrier, the stark reality hit me that the Marines are a division of the US Navy and, by signing up for the Navy, I was basically signing up for the Marine Corp. The military doesn't care that you're in the Navy. You are a soldier. They are going to give you a gun, and you are going to do what they tell you to do, wherever they want you to do it. They wanted me in the jungles of Vietnam and soon.

My beautiful dream was collapsing around me. I could feel it. I could see it. No more shiny shoes and spit clean decks, cruising the open waters of the Pacific Ocean living it up in exotic countries. Our unit was heading into the heart of the beast and I knew the wonderful life I had created in my mind with Leilani was shattering like a glass vase before my eyes.

No one put a gun to my head to sign the contract. It was my fault; I didn't read the fine print. I had no one to blame but myself for letting my father trick me into this nightmare. Hadn't he done enough to me and my brother? Why would he let me get roped into this?

It didn't matter anymore. I didn't matter anymore. Leilani didn't matter anymore. I was on my way to Hell and there was nothing anybody could do about it at this point.

I found out very quickly how efficient the bureaucracy of the United States government could be, especially in times of war. A brief trip through Camp Pendleton where I learned how to "Think like a Marine" and got a refresher course on how to navigate a swift boat, then it was off to Cue Viet Marine Corp Base along the Thach Han River in Vietnam. There was more training, spending six months there studying the waterways and geography of Vietnam. Finally, I was shipped overnight from Cue Viet to Bihn Thuy Air Force Base for more government "training."

That's when everything changed.

I was barely twenty years old, and the Marines had assigned me to drive a riverboat with four other soldiers onboard. We were on the Mekong River Delta every day hunting North Vietnamese soldiers fleeing into the neutral countries of Cambodia and Laos, and we were assigned to bring back dead and wounded American soldiers to basecamp. If you've ever seen the movie *Apocalypse Now*, when Martin Sheen was driving a boat up the river; that's exactly what I was doing.

As our riverboat chugged up the Mekong Delta, we would occasionally pass by boats similar to the one I was commandeering, half sunk with their tail ends sticking up out of the water, knowing full well they had hit a landmine the North Vietnamese Army had hidden in the river. It was a floating graveyard. I knew the remnants of those buried in the river were guys just like me. No one survived those attacks. I made a sign of the cross as we passed the floating graveyards and said a prayer hoping to God that wouldn't be our fate. It was my mission to *not* go out like that. There was no way I was going to let anything happen to my crew, so I was hyper vigilant as I scoured the water in front of me for landmines.

In war you develop a weird sixth sense, almost an intuition of when something bad is going to happen. It was going off in my head like a church bell. Our platoon typically slithered up the river under the cover of darkness for obvious reasons. It was an ungodly hour early morning. Harrowing silence. The only real light was the full moon bouncing off the reflection of the water.

We were only on the Mekong Delta about two days into my first trip up the river, when out of nowhere we started taking incoming fire. The sound of bullets buzzing past me affirmed my intuition. I immediately hit the gas to get our team out of range from the enemy's gunfire, and in the process, I hit a sandbar in the river. A sandbar! I promised myself I would never hit a sandbar, but in war almost everything is out of your control. As soon as the boat crashed into the sandbar, I went flying off the deck into the river cracking my head on a rock, knocking myself unconscious.

Everything after that was a blur. I vaguely remember a giant hand grabbing me by the collar, yanking me out of the water and pulling me back onto the boat. My focus came back into view on the deck of the boat as I stared vacantly up into the moonlit sky, as I noticed my best friend O'Reilly turn away from me shooting blindly into the jungle.

As I came to my senses, I realized O'Reilly had jumped off the boat into the river to save me. Now it was my turn to save him. The screams of my shipmates told me what I had to do. "GET THE DAMN BOAT OFF THE SANDBAR!" Everyone on the boat was busy returning fire into the unknown darkness. The boat was stuck, I was the captain, they were my crew and best friends, but I barely knew where I was as the ringing in my head drowned out the noise and chaos coming from the insanity around me.

I jumped up trying to gather my wits and make my way to the steering wheel controls. Before I could thank O'Reilly on my way to the front of the boat, I felt what I could only describe as warm milk splashing across my face. I wiped my face off only to realize that it was blood from O'Reilly. He had saved me again! He stood between me and the enemy fire providing cover, blocking the bullets from hitting me so I could get to the front of the boat and save the team. He had been shot in the head and collapsed onto the deck of the boat. I managed to maneuver the boat off the sandbar and hightail it out of enemy range.

"How could I have let this happen! How could I be so careless!" I kept churning these thoughts over and over in my head. O'Reilly's death would haunt me for years to come. I couldn't forgive myself for allowing this to happen and blamed myself for the death of my best friend who saved my life two times. His selfless acts of bravery stayed with me for the rest of my life.

War is hell, but it can bring out the best and worst in humanity as I would later find out. For the next two years of the war my soul shut down.

The letters from Leilani slowly diminished from what was a weekly flood to barely a drizzle to a total drought. Her letters just stopped coming. I knew it was over. The dream I had created with her morphed into what was now my nightmare in Vietnam. I couldn't keep up the façade. Instead of writing a long dear Leilani letter, I just stopped writing. It was the only way in my mind I was going to survive the brutality of the war. I told myself if I could have survived my childhood and make it this far alive, I could survive whatever we were doing in Vietnam.

The endless nightmare of the war continued for two more years up and down the river until that lucky day finally arrived in November 1969.

Chapter Three

ALOHA MY LOVE

What we have once enjoyed we can never lose. All that we love deeply becomes a part of us.

~ *Helen Keller*

My official discharge from the Marines came through and the military dumped me back into Honolulu. Only twenty-two, I had lived and died a few lifetimes in the war. Honolulu was different, America was different, I was different. Time seemed to stand still for the four years during my tours in Vietnam, and I somehow thought I was going to parachute back into Leilani's life as if nothing had ever happened. We would pick up right where we left off in our letters. I would find out very quickly what the war had done to me – to us.

I got in touch with my old running mate from back before I left for Vietnam and we fell back into our old ways tearing through the bars of Honolulu, only this time the drinking had a different meaning to it. It had a purpose. I was drowning out the pain and suffering I experienced during the war. I didn't know how else to deal with it. We carried on for a few months like this; all the while I was scouring Honolulu looking for Leilani – all to no avail.

I was starting to lose all hope when by pure chance one day I bumped into Leilani's sister at the supermarket. She and I were pretty close while I was living in Honolulu and dating Leilani. She didn't recognize me, so I approached her warily. "Hey Sheila, it's me, Freddie Clemett," I said in a low voice so as to not startle her in any way. She turned and looked at me, pausing as if she'd just seen a ghost. I could see in her eyes her brain trying to register if she knew this person standing in front of her.

After a few seconds I saw the light come on in her eyes and suddenly she threw her arms around me giving me a great big hug. "Oh my God, Freddie, I can't believe it's you!" she cried out. We embraced for what seemed like an eternity.

"Where have you been?" she asked.

"I was in Vietnam," I told her.

"You've been there this whole time? You left like four years ago?"

"Yeah, I can't believe it's been four years. I did two years on a carrier and two years in country. I'm so glad we bumped into each other; I've been looking all over Honolulu for Leilani. Is she still living on the west side?" I asked, almost begging for an answer.

By the change of the expression on her face I knew my luck had run out. "Freddie, I don't know how to tell you this; but after you stopped writing, we thought you died, and Leilani moved to Maui. She's married now and has a little baby girl."

I was speechless. I instantly went back to that dark void inside myself where I shut down every emotion to survive in Vietnam. In my mind, I was just burying another comrade and that part of my life right then and there.

"Well, tell her I said hello; just wanted to catch up on old times," I told Sheila nonchalantly hiding my devastation.

"She's gonna be so surprised to find out you're alive. Where are you staying in Honolulu?" she asked hesitantly.

"I'm actually leaving tomorrow – just here for a few days, but tell her I said hello and send my regards," I said, rushing to end the awkwardness of the moment. We exchanged pleasantries and I left as quickly as I arrived.

I went to the closest travel agency, booked a flight to New York City for early morning the next day, and called my brother Lloyd letting him know I would be staying with him for a while.

Chapter Four

JUST WHEN THINGS WERE GOING GREAT...

> Cast but a glance at riches, and they are gone, for they will surely sprout wings and fly off to the sky like an eagle.
>
> ~ *Proverbs 23:5 5*

I hit the ground running in New York. With Vietnam and my hopes for a life with Leilani in Honolulu in the rear-view mirror of my life, there was nothing standing in my way and no one was going to stop me.

A tiny ad in the New York Times for a salesman's position at the men's clothing company Barneys grabbed my attention. I was going to build an empire for myself no matter what I had to do to get it.

Within two years I was the top salesman at Barneys and thought I could really plant a flag within the organization and move my way up the ladder. But fate, as she has a tendency to do, had other plans for me. Barneys hired a new manager and he had different ideas for the organization and my role in it. Within six months of him getting hired I was out of a job.

After all I had been through, this minor obstacle wasn't going to hold me back. I had built a stable and loyal clientele throughout my two years at Barneys and had a great reputation with them. One day I ran into one of my former clients in Manhattan and he mentioned that he hadn't seen me around at Barneys recently. I told him the new manager had made some drastic changes and I was one of them. He immediately handed me his business card and told me about a good friend of his who was a Hollywood producer and was building a clothing line. He thought I would be a great fit for the company. I thanked him and called the contact a few days later. Before I knew it, I was working for Evan Picone, managing six states in their southwest territory.

Once someone finds their calling and connects with it on a spiritual level, I believe there is no stopping them. I found mine – I was a garment salesman and one of the best in the business. My numbers proved it.

My mother always told me to strike while the iron is hot. So I took the leap of faith and, after a couple of years with Evan Picone, I started my own company as a manufacturer's representative carrying clothing lines with twenty different brand names throughout the Southwest. The business took off like a rocket. Everything was falling into place on a career level.

Once again, Cupid struck me down. While traveling in Dallas, I was at a department store that was carrying a few of my clothing lines and one of the salesclerks wandered over to help me setup my displays. Her name was Jenny, and I saw the same glowing aura surrounding her as I had seen with Leilani. Those same feelings I had for Leilani started to well up within me again, and five years later I was happily married to her, raising two daughters, and making money hand over fist. I was buying real estate in and around the Dallas Fort Worth area. I couldn't lose. I was on a winning streak. But nothing lasts forever, and the foundation of my perfect life and business empire was starting to crumble under my feet.

I was burning the midnight oil seven days a week working eighteen hour days building my company. It may have been my idea of getting there, but it wasn't my wife's. She was home raising the kids by herself and, although I was providing food on the table and then some, she needed me to be there both for her and the kids. Even when I was there physically, I wasn't there emotionally.

About four years into our marriage, I started having flashbacks about my time in Vietnam. I had been out of the jungles for years and the war was a distant memory – or so I thought. Now it was coming back again with a vengeance. I'd never experienced anything like this in my life. My anger was explosive; any little thing set me off. I was having severe nightmares and flashbacks reliving the horrors of my time in the war. I could barely sleep, and when I did, I slept with a loaded .45 caliber on my nightstand. I started sleeping fully clothed fearing that at any moment I would have to spring out of bed and shoot at the enemy breaking into my home. This was the onset of Post-Traumatic Stress Disorder (PTSD), but I didn't even know at the time what it was.

Often problems in life come in waves and I wasn't immune to this. In addition to dealing with my mental and emotional collapse, I was trying to manage my deteriorating relationship with my wife and kids, juggle a multimillion-dollar real estate portfolio, and run a clothing company with 25 employees.

Then the earthquake hit. It was the mid 80s and, seemingly overnight, the bottom fell out in the real estate market in Dallas. A crushing recession hit, which lasted for the next eight years. It seemed like everything vanished overnight.

The feelings and symptoms of PTSD were getting continuously worse and I started drinking heavily again.

There are some moments in life that you never forget. Sitting at my kitchen table signing my divorce papers, then signing my bankruptcy papers and losing everything I had worked for over the past ten years all in the same month were two of those moments. I lingered around the house for a few weeks drinking myself into oblivion to numb the pain as my wife packed up the kids to move in with her parents in Houston.

After the house was sold, I lived out of my car for another couple of months, aimlessly drifting and driving around Dallas lamenting the events of my life. My ultimate demise seemed not too far off and I knew if I stayed in Dallas I was a goner. It was too painful. Too much wreckage. If I was going to be there for my family, I knew I had to rebuild my life and go somewhere where I wouldn't be judged and have unconditional love. My brother Lloyd was my only hope, so I got myself on the earliest flight to New York City...again.

Chapter Five

PHOENIX RISING

> Our greatest glory is not in never falling, but in rising every time we fall.
>
> ~ *Confucius*

Lloyd had been sixteen years sober, and after what he had been through in his life, it was a miracle he was still alive. That's why I admired him so much: he was a fighter. I laid it down to him what was going on with me – the bankruptcy, the PTSD, the drinking, the divorce – everything. He introduced me to one of his friends who was a veteran from Vietnam and was getting help from the Veterans Administration to deal with his own PTSD. I immediately got plugged in with the VA and was diagnosed with a severe case of PTSD. Now, everything in my life was starting to make sense – the flashbacks, the mood swings, the depression.

I dived into my recovery headfirst with my eyes closed. I knew I had been given a second chance at life and I wasn't going to blow it. I quit drinking, got into a twelve-step program, made amends with my wife and kids back in Dallas, started counseling sessions twice a week at the VA, and got active in support groups with veterans suffering from PTSD.

Al the same, I knew I needed to stay in New York City for a while to get better, so I did what I knew to do best:

Shined my shoes
Put on my best suit
Put a smile on my face
Combed my hair
Hit the pavement and went to work

I did whatever it took to get my life back. I took the first job I could get as a stock clerk replenishing shelves in a supermarket. I didn't care; I wasn't going to let my ego and pride get in the way of rebuilding my life. Every day I gave it 110 percent, knowing my next opportunity was just around the corner; I just had to keep putting one foot in front of the other and stay consistent doing the work I needed to do.

I still had some connections in the garment industry, so I started my business back up as a manufacturer's representative all the while working forty hours a week at the grocery store and keeping up with my meetings and groups. It was a heck of a struggle. I was grinding it out day in and day out for two straight years barely coming up for air. But gradually the clutter started to clear. I was soon able to quit my stock clerk job and focus on the clothing consulting company full time. Next to surviving Vietnam and my collapse in Dallas, this was the hardest time in my life, but I knew if I kept pushing forward it would be well worth it.

A much needed vacation to celebrate my new life and avoid burnout made a lot of sense, so I carved out a couple of days for a quick getaway to Miami. While boarding the airplane for Florida, Cupid struck again. An attractive young woman accidentally misread her boarding pass and was sitting in my seat. Not being the shy type, I struck up a conversation and ten months later we were madly in love, married, and living in a small apartment on Christopher Street in Greenwich Village. With the help of a lot of people and an enormous amount of hard work and commitment, I had recreated my life.

I was a man on a mission rising out of the ashes like a Phoenix. I devoured everything I could to take me to the next level and change my life. I knew it started in my mind, as most things do, and my attitude and perspective were critical to building the foundation of my future life. I immersed myself in all the positive thinking literature I could get my hands on. Some were worthless, some weren't. Some were revolutionary. I read everything from Confucius to Marcus Aurelius to Nietzsche to Plato. My studies spanned the history of mankind's greatest thinkers. I studied all the great religions – Buddhism, Islam, Hinduism, Jainism, Christianity, Judaism, even some I couldn't pronounce. Nothing was too esoteric or off limits.

I wasn't going to let this opportunity for a new life slip through my fingers. I kept up with my twelve-step recovery program diligently. Exercise was almost a religion.

After several years of absolute and total dedication, determination, discipline, patience and an enormous amount of hard work along with the help of my loving and loyal wife and a lot of kind and generous people, I stepped out a new man.

Then I got the call.

CHRIS'S STORY

Chapter Six

MY TURBULENT YOUTH

> A life without purpose is a languid, drifting thing; every day we ought to review our purpose, saying to ourselves: This day let me make a sound beginning, for what we have hitherto done is naught!
>
> ~ *Thomas à Kempis*

I grew up in what you would call a middle to lower middle-class household, I guess. It wasn't for lack of effort on my parents' part. My mother was a kindergarten teacher, and my father was an airline pilot. They were good supportive parents – Norman Rockwell stuff. As a child I didn't know and couldn't have cared less about my family's socioeconomic background. I just wanted to enjoy sports, play video games and have acorn fights with my friends.

As early as I can remember, my father was never home; he was always working. He was an airline pilot with TWA and opened an auto parts store on the side. In case things didn't work out with the airlines, he would have something for his wife and four kids to fall back on.

I was around ten years old when the Rockwell painting started to melt. It was 1979 and the gas crisis hit America hard and people stopped flying. Within the course of eighteen months, my father was laid off from the airlines, his auto parts store burned to the ground and he had a massive heart attack one week after his health insurance expired. There he was: forty-two years old, no job, his business burned down, and in desperate need of open-heart surgery. Our family was devastated, and we didn't know what to do.

Back in those days, media was very different than today. We had only three TV channels, no internet, no cellphone, and most people had one phone line at home, usually a rotary phone. There were no answering or caller ID machines at that time either. When the phone rang someone in the house ran to answer it, and it was usually me.

My father had borrowed against our house to finance the auto parts store and, after he got laid off from the airlines, he subsequently had difficulty paying the mortgage. Banks would call our house phone threatening to foreclose on our property and throw us out onto the streets. As a ten-year-old answering the phone, hearing those threats, those dangers get deeply embedded in a young child's mind and stay with him for the rest of his life. I would have nightmares for years to come. To this day when I think about the struggles of my family as a child, a familiar darkness still clouds my mind.

We were in dire straits. Our family was on the verge of being homeless and at that tender age I knew the harsh reality we were facing. Impending financial collapse was mounting every day, and if my father didn't get the heart surgery immediately, he wasn't going to make it. The only problem was he didn't have health insurance and the surgery was over $100,000.

When I look back on the trajectory of my life, it is amazing how people have come into my life at times to help me at what appear to have been random coincidences. Were they random? I don't know, but they seem to have been orchestrated for my benefit.

One of our neighbors, who had just moved into our neighborhood from Pakistan, happened to be a vascular surgeon. He had contacts and relationships with a special heart hospital that provided free open -heart surgery. There was a two year waiting list, but our neighbor was able to get my father into the hospital for surgery within two weeks of his heart attack. The surgery was successful, but my father was never quite the same. I guess for some having such a dramatic experience changes you forever.

Our family started a long dark march out of poverty trying to climb back into the middle class. The aftermath for me was equally demanding. Dark spells of depression were affecting all areas of my life. My grades fell off and I started withdrawing from my social world. Around this time, I developed and was diagnosed with a reading comprehension deficit disorder compounded by a series of vastly different diagnoses for depression. These mental and emotional issues got progressively worse. My parents brought me in and out of psychiatrists' offices to work through what was going on in my life. Nothing helped.

I entered high school utterly insecure about who I was and what my life was going to be. I didn't feel like I fit in and wandered into the drinking and partying crowd. My freshman and sophomore years continued in this fashion and I would have failed out of high school had it not been for my sophomore English teacher Mr. O'Leary.

Right away he noticed my struggle with the reading assignments. He would meet with me during my lunch breaks to show me how to learn, memorize and comprehend the material I was studying. He taught me the Cornell method, a formal way to take notes and organize lectures. He taught me the Method of Loci, which was an ancient mnemonic technique the Roman and Greeks used to enhance their recall of subjects they studied, and he also encouraged me to get involved in sports. To this day I'm not sure why Mr. O'Leary went out of his way to help me, but without him, I don't know if I could have turned my life around. My grades started to get better, I was captain of the basketball team my senior year and the darkness of my early years seemed to dissipate as I headed off to college to begin a new season.

College was an amazing world: new friends, new knowledge, new experiences. For the first two years, it was a time of tremendous personal growth. Then the hard decisions had to be made. I had to pick a major and decide on what I was going to do in my career. The only problem was I was alone in my head and didn't have anyone to guide me. I had no idea fundamentally who I was and what I really wanted. So I drifted through college with no particular aim other than trying to get the best grades I could, thinking that they would carry me into a better place later on.

I graduated college and moved back in with my parents in New Jersey. I figured I could get a job in New York City and save money on rent while I commuted back and forth from the city. I got a job in North Jersey and was schlepping an hour each way to a forklift company where I was working as a shipping clerk. Six months into my stay at home, my father died of a stroke. I was lucky to have spent some time with him before his passing. But now I was lost again. This wasn't the idea of what my future would be, so after my father died, I figured I had nothing to lose and I packed my bags and headed to Southern California.

I drove across the country visiting some friends along the way. As soon as I crossed the border of California, my radiator blew out and I was driving around Los Angeles with only couple of gallons of water in my trunk pulling over every few hours to fill it up. This was ***definitely not*** the future I had planned for myself – living in a youth hostel and driving around a busted- up Chevy Celebrity in Venice California trying to figure out what to do with my life.

After a few months of endless drifting in California, it was time to regroup. I sold my car, put my tail between my legs and headed back to New Jersey to see if I could try my luck getting a job in New York City again. After a series of failed sales jobs commuting an hour and a half each way back and forth into the city,

I moved in with a friend of mine from high school, and got a job as a waiter in the theater district to pay my bills.

While my friends were getting married, raising families, and building careers, here I was at twenty-eight years old, living with two roommates at 238th Street and Broadway in the Bronx, working as a waiter trying to "figure" out my life and manage my depression, hoping and praying I wouldn't run into anyone I went to high school with. My battered self-image and self-esteem only exacerbated the situation.

If I did by any chance run into anyone I knew from school days, I had the perfect alibi as to why I was working as a waiter: I would drop the struggling actor routine on them and, hopefully, that would excuse away the failure of my life as a waiter at twenty eight years old. Later on in life I would be introduced to the twenty, forty, sixty concept. It goes like this: "When I was twenty I cared what people thought about me, when I was forty, I didn't care what people thought about me, and when I was sixty, I realized nobody was thinking about me in the first place." At this period in my life, however, I was deeply concerned about what I thought people were thinking about me, as naïve as that seems now.

Chapter Seven

FORTUNE KNOCKS

Sometimes the greatest adventure is a simple conversation.

~ Amadeus Mozart

Fortune finally smiled. It was a typically crazy night at the restaurant, and I was running around like a madman trying to get the food out on time to all my tables. A waiter I was working with had got sick and asked me if I could take over his shift. I reluctantly agreed. As I approached one of his tables, I noticed two guys around my age with at least $2000 worth of top- shelf bottles of booze scattered across their table. It seemed they were having the time of their lives.

As I got closer, I recognized one of them as someone I went to high school with. Before I could make the quickest u-turn possible, he recognized me and shouted my name across the room, "HEY CHRIS! HOW ARE YOU! IT'S ME BRAD FROM CHEMISTRY CLASS!" Through the grapevine I heard Brad was making an absolute ton of money working on Wall Street and I didn't want him to see me carrying around plates of failure to ungrateful diners. I was about to drop the struggling actor routine, but before I could, he blurted out, "Hey ya know, I used to work here to pay my way through college. Does Tony still own the place?"

This caught me off guard a bit; I didn't know he had worked at the same restaurant.

"Yeah he does," I replied.

"He's quite the character, isn't he?" Brad laughed.

"Yeah he's something else," I said. I was starting to feel a little less insecure about wearing a clip-on bow tie with my second-hand tuxedo, knowing Brad had done the same and was now a big shot on Wall Street. Maybe there was hope for me after all.

"You should come work with me, do what I do," he said casually.

"What's that?" I asked.

He pointed to the bottles on the table and said, "Can you do this?"

"What...drink?" I asked.

"Pretty much, yeah. Drink and go out to dinner anywhere you want, whenever you want at the best bars and restaurants in the city. That's basically what I do," he replied with a grin.

I thought about it for a moment, "Yeah I think I can do that."

"OK, give me a call I'll hook you up with a job." He handed me a business card and told me to call him the next day. I took the card, thanked him and made my way as fast as I could back into the kitchen, so I wouldn't have to continue with the tortuous small talk at the table.

The next day I was on the phone talking to Brad. The following Monday I was interviewing with a hard charging Wall Street executive named Karen who ran the currency trading desk handling forwards and options in Latin America. I had no idea what they did, but I blabbered on about how much the stock market interested me. She kept telling me this wasn't the stock market – it was the currency market. I had no idea what the currency market was. Later I found out it was roughly ten times the size of the stock market, ran 24 hours a day, and handled over $7 trillion in transactions daily!

The sounds of the traders shouting orders across the trading floor wasn't helping my nervousness as Karen kept asking me to speak up because she couldn't hear me. I could tell the interview was heading south fast and Karen politely escorted me out of her office. I went to the trading desk where Brad was working.

"How did it go?" he asked.

"I don't think I got it, to be honest. I don't think she liked me too much," I told him.

Behind Brad a broker was talking on the phone in Spanish to a trader on a currency desk in Mexico. The broker told a joke in Spanish into the phone and I started laughing. I was far from fluent in Spanish, but four years in college, a semester abroad in Mexico and a two-year relationship with a girl from Barcelona could get me around enough to get into trouble.

"Do me a favor. Can you tell that joke to my client?" Brad asked me.

He walked past Karen and picked up the phone. Trading desk phones don't dial, they have automatic connections to execute trades instantaneously. He put me on the phone with his client, one of the largest traders of Mexican Pesos on the largest trading desk in Mexico. I told him the joke across the phone in Spanish and he started cracking up. Karen was standing right there and shot me a look that could melt ice. I knew she didn't want to hire me, but in that industry the traders are king. If they want the brokers to hire someone, they will; otherwise the brokers won't be getting any business from their trading desks, which ranged in the tens of millions of dollars. Brad took the phone from my hand and gave it to Jackie. The trader in Mexico told her to hire me. I started the following Monday.

I had done it. I hit the jackpot. Just twenty-eight and working on one of the largest currency trading desks at one of the most prestigious brokerage firms on Wall Street! Everyone on the desk was under thirty-five and easily pulling down five hundred thousand to $1 million a year in commissions.

The first three months were a dream. Just like Brad had said, we were out every night at the best bars and clubs, limos, and everything else that came with that lifestyle. I had taken a bite of the glamour of the Big Apple, and I couldn't believe my good fortune.

The only thing was the problem with depression. It doesn't care about what is going on in your external world; it will strike regardless of the good and positive things going on in your life and bring you to your knees.

After about nine months I was done. Despite having "arrived" on Wall Street, it was over as quickly as it started. No more dreams of financial glory. I couldn't take it anymore. I was just too burned out, and stopped going to work. The commute was killing me, taking two trains from the Bronx all the way down to Wall Street. We had to be in the office at 7:00 am every day and we left at 5:00 pm. Then it was out all night schmoozing traders and partying in the hope of getting some deals for the next day. I typically didn't get home from "work" until three or four in the morning. After so many nights, it became untenable and it was just easier to bring a few suits to work and sleep under my desk so I wouldn't be late. The partying was killing me; the lack of sleep was brutal. On top of that my depression had come back with a vengeance and was tormenting me. Bad career choice!

I had no idea what to do next. I was dying on the inside and having a hard time getting out of bed. I needed to make money as the bills were piling up. So I took the first job I could get my hands on, working at a moving company.

One minute I was working as a waiter in the theater district hoping and praying no one I knew would recognize me. The next minute I was sitting on one of the largest currency trading desks on Wall Street surrounded by young millionaires trading hundreds of millions of dollars in currency contracts daily. And now I was crammed into a tiny moving truck sandwiched between two off the boat Irishmen who would pull over whenever they got the chance to duck into the nearest Starbucks bathroom to shoot heroin. ***Definitely not*** the life I'd planned!

That nightmare continued for a few months until another random encounter changed my direction once again. I was sitting next to a very attractive woman on the subway and struck up a conversation. I summoned the words to speak to her – though not from some great reservoir of confidence because my self-esteem was so crushed it couldn't go any lower, and I literally didn't care what she said. As my stop was rapidly approaching, I marshaled the courage to ask her out on a date. She politely told me she was in a serious relationship but did have a friend named Marie who she thought I might want to talk to. I got her phone number and three weeks later Marie and I were best friends taking a computer class together. Marie had been in the computer field for many years and talked me into taking a class with her to learn about the newest Microsoft operating system. The moving gig was absolutely killing me, so I figured this might be an opportunity to change my life once again.

I dived into studying computers more out of fear of failure and being stuck at the moving company than out of any real interest in the technology itself. From there I talked my way into a temp job basically doing secretarial work and minor Microsoft office tasks for different executives at an investment bank. About four months into my temp job, someone left the computer department within the bank, and I threw myself at the mercy of the hiring manager. It didn't hurt that I had been working directly for one of the highest level executives in the company and she was able to put in a good word for me.

The computer business started a whole new path for me at twenty-nine. My self-esteem and hope for my life were back on forward track. Within two years working the help desk job at the bank, I parlayed my computer skills into a managerial position at a pharmaceutical company. I finally secured a corporate executive position managing the entire IT department for the New York office of a global advertising company reporting to the Chief Operating Officer. I got an apartment in Manhattan and felt like I was back on top of the world.

Once again, a fateful event, this time a random call to Hewlett Packard, would alter the course of my life. I needed to purchase some computer equipment for the New York office, so I called Hewlett Packard to find a local dealer. HP corporate gave me three numbers of local dealers in New York City. The first one didn't pick up the phone, the second said he would call me back but never did, and the third one I fell in love with. The moment we spoke I felt something different. We connected immediately. She came to my office the following day and knocked me off my chair. Dark flowing jet-black hair, with walnut brown eyes, she glided into my office with the grace of a ballet dancer. I couldn't take my eyes off her. I never felt I could connect with women emotionally, let alone a spiritual level. With her it was totally different. Before I knew it, we were living together, I quit my job with the advertising company, and I was partnering with her to help build her technology company in New York City.

I felt I had reached another pinnacle in my life destined to go higher. Here I was, a business owner with an office on Wall Street, an apartment on Wall Street, in love and living together with my girlfriend who happened to be my business partner. Awesome!

Over the course of the next seven years, we built the business to thirty-three employees with clients in three states. I had arrived again – or so I thought. I would soon find out life has a funny way of turning the tide on our best laid plans. After seven years of my dream life, cracks began to appear in the veneer. The stress was starting to weigh me down, and I started drinking again to deal with the pressure.

My business partner and now fiancée and I fought about everything. When you live together and work together, things can become incredibly difficult. We were together twenty-four hours a day for weeks on end. Here you are in business making hundreds of decisions on a daily basis about everything – from hiring/firing employees, the new and next marketing plan, to deciding whether to upgrade the accounting software. The decisions were endless. There was so much tension between us we couldn't even agree on the shade of blue for the new business cards.

And all along my depression was deepening. Eventually I moved out of our apartment and got my own place showing up less and less to work. The writing was on the wall. I just didn't read it or didn't want to read it. Everything we had built together over the past seven years was cascading for a collapse.

Chapter Eight

FACE TO FACE WITH FREDDIE

> The connections we make in the course of a life – maybe that's what heaven is.
>
> ~ *Mr. Rogers*

In spite of my "Rome is burning" situation, an unanticipated opportunity fell in my lap. One of my employees introduced me to a friend of his who was interested in starting a software educational company designed to teach math to children through games and social interactions on a web portal. A similar kind of software had recently been sold to Disney for hundreds of millions of dollars, so the idea was appealing. Besides, I needed something I could throw myself into to take my mind off the world crumbling around me.

My business partner and fiancée had recently moved to Switzerland to live with her aunt to try and "find herself." I wasn't surprised; our relationship had slowly deteriorated over the past years and I was in a strange way glad to see her go. Maybe at least one of us could squeeze some happiness out of this life.

We tried to keep the business running with her living in another part of the world and me grinding it out in New York City. Sales were lagging and we were losing customers. My partner and I were 4,000 miles apart and fighting about everything all the time. So when the opportunity came to move in a totally different direction with a new team of people on an entirely new project, I swarmed all over it.

The idea was simple. We would develop interactive software with cartoon characters and a dedicated portal to teach young children math. Our team couldn't have been more impressive – at least on paper to accomplish that goal. One of the partners Steve owned a chain of preschools. The other Amir was from India and had fantastic contacts there that could develop the software at an incredibly low price. I had the technology, technical expertise and connections to support and manage the software on the backend. The front-end user interface would be developed in India. We would create the characters together here in the States with a cartoonist in New York City, and would continue to monitor and manage the progress as a team until the prototype was completed.

We each put in $10,000 for an even 10% equity stake for each partner. We allocated another 10% for charitable purposes and the remaining 60% equity for investors later on in the project. Amir assured us that $30,000 would be enough for us to develop at least thirty minutes of programming. After that, we would have a viable prototype and could either raise money to finish it or sell off what we had. Seemed reasonable enough to me.

Amir came to us with the idea for the software. He was essentially running the project because most of the initial work was being done in India. He lived there part of the year, and with technology being seamlessly global, we didn't care. Everything started out wonderfully. We developed the first ten minutes of the software and it was stunning. I knew we had a homerun.

We were all excited about our progress on the project. However, things, as they have a tendency to do, started changing rather quickly. I could tell something was wrong. We were regularly scheduling conference calls even when he was traveling in India and all of a sudden they stopped. Amir would sporadically send emails on updates and new coding ideas here and there, but the continuity and momentum had come to a screeching halt.

After months of wrangling and cajoling, the three of us finally scheduled an in-person meeting at my office in New York City – with a twist. My partner Steve who ran the preschools, brought along a friend of his, a man named Freddie Clemett, to help us work out our arrangement with Amir going forward since we weren't having any luck ourselves. I figured we had nothing to lose, so I agreed. At this point I didn't care anymore. I was exhausted with my life and could use all the help I could get.

We all arrived at the office thirty minutes before the scheduled meeting with Amir to discuss what we were going to talk about. Freddie entered the room like a Rockstar; dressed to the nines and radiating confidence and enthusiasm. He was wearing a navy-blue Armani suit with a burgundy red power tie. His hair was white and flowing and not a hair out of place. It reminded me of a lion's mane. Freddie was about 5'6" tall, but he had such an aura around him, when I think of first meeting him my memory was of him being taller than me. I am 6'3". He had that kind of energy about him. We hit it off right away.

"Hiya doin, Chris, Freddie Clemett, nice to meet you," Freddie said with a giant smile, his teeth as white as snow. He reached out his hand to shake mine. I shook his hand and it felt like it was in a vice grip.

"Nice to meet you, Freddie; I've heard a lot about you," I told him.

"Tell me what's going on?" he asked me.

"Well, we're having some problems with Amir. This software project is stalled and we need to figure out what we're going to do next. We've built the introduction, but it hasn't moved forward since that," I explained.

"No...I mean what's going on with you, Chris? How's your life?" Freddie asked.

I knew Freddie was there to help us get the software project resolved, but he was asking about me personally. Besides the army of psychologists I had been going to in the past few years, no one really seemed to care that much. So I gave him the standard answer that I gave everyone who asked me.

"I'm doing great; thanks for asking. How are you? How was your trip?" A little trick I learned in my sales career was to constantly get the clients talking about their own interests and what they wanted. Everyone likes to talk about themselves.

Freddie threw me a smile. He knew what I was up to and he played my game. "Good, I had a great flight from Dallas to see my family and I'm glad to be back in New York. Now tell me what's going on with the software you're working on. Steve filled me in on some of the details, and I wanted to hear your side of the story. Get your perspective on what's going on," he said matter-of-factly.

I filled him in on our progress, or lack thereof, and he just patiently listened and nodded his head in agreement. The three of us put our game plan together right before Amir showed up.

Amir was a little startled at having Freddie present in the meeting since we didn't tell him Freddie was coming. But we proceeded as planned. Freddie introduced himself to Amir as a good friend of Steve's, who had invited him here to see if he could help fix some of the issues they were facing.

"Sure," Amir said uneasily, as if Freddie had found out a secret about him. Amir proceeded to give us his sales pitch on how the project was coming along, all the wonderful things that were happening in India and how much money we were going to make. He rambled on for about half an hour before Freddie abruptly interrupted him.

"How much you want?" Freddie blurted out.

"Excuse me?" Amir said almost apologetically.

"How much you want? I assume you are here to ask for more money; is that right? Is that why you haven't been getting back to your two business partners here who put their trust in you and gave you their hard- earned money to develop this software?" Freddie asked bluntly.

"Everything is going great, trust me. If you would just let me finish my presentation we can discuss what we need to go forward," retorted Amir.

Freddie wasn't budging. He knew Amir's game. "Look Amir, you promised your partners you would have thirty minutes of fully developed software with their money and I only see barely ten minutes. How much do you need, Amir?" Freddie asked again. He had a way of getting right to the point and bypassing all the nonsense.

Amir was filibustering trying to bring us back to his well-oiled presentation obviously designed to pull more money out of our pockets. But he knew he was cornered in a dead end, and finally gave in.

"I need another 30 grand to get the thirty-minute tape finished," he said timidly.

"30 thousand? I think we're done here," Freddie said politely as he got up from the table and quietly left.

The three of us just kind of sat in the office not knowing what to make of what had just transpired. We tried to make awkward conversation, and Amir asked if we would watch the rest of the presentation, but I was exhausted and didn't feel like sticking around much longer. I got up and told Chris and Amir it would be better if we continued the discussion the next day, and we left my office.

Bright and early the next morning at 9:00 am my phone rang. It was a strange number and I was hesitant to answer.

"Hello," I answered cautiously.

"Hey Chris, it's Freddie Clemett, how ya doin today?"

I was surprised to hear from him. "Pretty good, how ya doin Freddie?"

"Quite an interesting night we had last night, huh?" he remarked.

"That was quite the show you put on," I told him.

"Listen, I've seen thousands of guys like Amir. I knew what he was up to; that's why I cut the meeting short. I got a great BS meter and I can sense it a mile away. I was just bluffing, but I wanted to see how he would react. I know Steve is going out of town for the weekend, but maybe we can meet up tomorrow to discuss how you want to proceed? I haven't been to the Palm Restaurant for a long time. Why don't you meet me there? We can get something to eat and talk a little bit more about this software you're developing and see what we can do with this partner of yours."

I was very content to avoid the scope of my reality and hide under the covers on a Friday night, so I tried to tap-dance around the issue. "I don't know," I began, "Friday night, it's gonna be crowded and I'm gonna be exhausted. It's been a long week," I said, trying to talk my way out of it.

"Come on, it's Friday night. Let's get something to eat at the Palm...trust me; they got the best steaks in town. I'm buying," Freddie said. Persistence, I was later to find out, was a defining characteristic of Freddie. I could tell he wasn't going to let me off the hook, so I conceded.

"OK, what time are you thinking?" I asked.

"Meet me over there around 7:30 and we'll catch up. Look forward to seeing you there, Chris!" Freddie said cheerfully.

"OK, I'll see you at 7:30 tomorrow at the Palm," I replied reluctantly.

Chapter Nine

SEE THE LIFE RAFT

There Are No Strangers Here; Only Friends You Haven't Yet Met.

~ *William Butler Yeats*

Friday night rolled around and I really wasn't in the mood to meet up with Freddie. My depression was crushing me and the last thing I wanted to do was wage war with my two arch nemeses: crowds of people and making small talk with strangers. The thought of barricading myself in my room, losing myself in a gallon of Haagen Daz mint chocolate chip ice cream and watching reruns of old Seinfeld episodes was much more appealing. But somehow I forced myself to get out of bed and get to the Palm. Maybe Freddie could help me get this software problem resolved. One less headache to deal with. Besides, a nice steak might do me good.

I arrived at the Palm and the wall of noise from the crowd hit me like a tidal wave. I had to summon everything within me not to turn and run as fast and as far as I could from the restaurant. The place was packed. I could barely hear my thoughts over the roar of conversations and overly loud Italian opera blasting in the background. Caricatures of famous cultural icons splattered the walls as the waiters with their tan overcoats and black ties shouted above the clamor to the patron what was on the menu. The Palm didn't have written menus and was notoriously expensive.

Freddie and I spotted each other from across the room, and he waved me over to the bar where he was holding court with three strangers, Wall Street executives of some sort, I'm sure. They were spellbound by his stories and he kept everyone in stitches. There was something about Freddie people took a liking to instantly. I made my way to the bar as he shook my hand and slapped me on the back as if he hadn't seen me in twenty years.

"Hey Chris, great to see ya!" he shouted above the racket of the restaurant. He introduced me to his newfound friends, and I forced the best "Hello" I could muster given my state of mind. I flagged the bartender down and ordered a vodka tonic. After a few minutes of mindless banter with the strangers at the bar, I was glad when the waitress stopped by with my drink and let Freddie know our table was ready.

"Guys, you'll have to excuse me, I have a reservation with my friend Chris here. It's been nice talking with you," he said as he reached into his wallet and dropped a fifty dollar bill on the bar, letting the bartender know he would be picking up the next round of drinks for his friends. The bar erupted into a resounding round of applause. We excused ourselves and made our way to the back of the restaurant.

We sat down at our table and Freddie didn't miss a beat. "So how did it go with Amir after I left?" he asked.

"It was awkward, I didn't stay too long. He tried to get back into his sales pitch but I was too tired to hear the same story line. I did talk to him earlier today briefly," I said.

"What did he say?" Freddie inquired.

"He was tap dancing around the money just like he was doing with you yesterday."

He nodded. "You got a great product from what I've seen so far, but that guy's not shooting straight with you."

"Yeah, I know, I'm starting to get a bad feeling about this situation. What do you think we should do?" I asked.

"I'm working on some ideas. I'll give you a call during the week and we can jump on a conference call with Steve to discuss it," he said.

"That sounds like a plan," I answered.

"How are things going with the computer company? Steve was telling me your girlfriend is opening an office in Switzerland?" he asked with a certain empathy.

"Well yeah, in a way, I guess. She's actually my fiancée. She moved in with her aunt and is figuring out her life from there. I'm trying to keep the business afloat while she's in Switzerland doing her thing," I said.

The waitress came by and took our order.

"They got the best porterhouse steaks in the city, trust me on that. I'll have mine medium rare. Chris how do you like your steak?" Freddie asked excitedly.

"I'll have the same," I said.

She asked if we wanted some drinks. Freddie raised his glass he brought back from the bar, lifted it up and shook it. "I'll have another seltzer water with a twist of lime, sweetheart," he said.

I ordered another vodka tonic.

"I see you like to throw back a few," said Freddie.

"Yeah kinda helps gets the monkey off my back," I mumbled.

"You're a young guy, Chris, with all your life in front of you. What kind of pain are you in?" he asked as he looked into my eyes.

I barely knew Freddie, but there was something about him that I felt I could trust. I could tell he was genuinely interested in what I was going through. Besides, it was kind of a relief to actually talk with someone about my life to whom I didn't have to pay $200 per hour and ask me relentless questions about my childhood.

"It's a long story," I said.

"We got some time. It's gonna be awhile before our steaks get here," he said reassuringly.

At this point I didn't care anymore. I was just going to be honest with Freddie and let him know straight up what was going on in my life.

"Aside from the fact she left me for Switzerland doing God only knows what, we just lost our best salesman, and it looks like he might be taking our biggest account with him. So now we are on the brink of officially losing money every month. If we don't make some changes quickly, we aren't going to be in business too much longer and this software thing with Amir isn't helping my mental state either," I lamented.

"And drinking is going to help you how?" Freddie asked kindly.

"It helps mask the pain."

"Extrapolate, Chris, extrapolate," he insisted.

"What do you mean?" I asked.

"If you keep doing what you're doing, where are you going to be in three, four, ten years? If you think you have problems now, keep drinking and all your problems will go away, along with everything else in your life. I got ten years sober. One of hardest things I've ever done in life but totally worth it. I live head-on with whatever comes my way. No masks, no crutches, no excuses, Chris."

"Yeah, that's probably the best way to live," I said halfheartedly.

"Just gotta commit, that's all it takes."

"I guess I could try. Life's just difficult to face head-on," I told him.

"That's the point. The only way out is through, and the only way through is to do the opposite. It's the only way to make changes in your life."

"I don't know if Steve ever told you but I did four tours in Vietnam," Freddie asked.

"No he didn't."

"Trust me, if you think you're in the darkest point of your life now and you have problems. Try being stuck 9,000 miles from home on a boat twelve feet long, in 110-degree weather, with total strangers, in a country where you don't speak the language, in pitch blackness. Picture bullets flying past you in every imaginable direction and you think everyone is trying to kill you and you don't know who the enemy is and who isn't. That's hopelessness. Oh, and the food was beyond horrible," he said as he leaned back in his chair and took a sip of his seltzer.

"Wow! I thought I was going through a hard time. That sounds beyond miserable," I said.

"You have no idea," Freddie replied. "First thing you gotta realize, Chris, is there is always an answer. There's always a way out. You can't see it now because you're in it. It's like you're drowning underwater and can't see the life raft floating above you. You gotta believe it's out there," he said with conviction. "You've told me a little about your story. You just need a little light to illuminate the way and a little help to show you how to get there."

"I dunno, I don't see any way out of this," I said.

"Your life isn't much different from mine. I survived the war, and worse, and I'm here sitting talking to you. I got a few scars along the way and left claw marks on everything I ever touched – but I made it through, and you can too. All you have to do at this point is believe there's a better life waiting for you, put one foot in front of the next, and ask for help. Listen, take my card, call me anytime. We'll get this software thing figured out, don't worry about that," he assured me.

I took Freddie's card and put it in my pocket just as the steaks were arriving. The smell of the sautéed steak and my conversation with Freddie helped quiet the noise in my head – at least for a little while.

Chapter Ten

ACCEPT YOUR REALITY

We cannot change anything unless we first accept it.

~ *Carl Jung*

About midweek I started to bottom out...again. I could barely drag myself out of bed to confront the pressures overwhelming me, so I decided to call Freddie and see if he'd made any progress with my software debacle. He greeted me on the phone with the same enthusiasm as when I first met him. I did my best to cover up the depression I was battling. I was pretty good at putting on my "face" to mask to the outside world what I was truly feeling. Early on in my sales career I learned people don't like to deal with people who seem depressed or down. When they go to Disneyland, they want to buy Mickey Mouse, not the depressed guy hiding underneath the mouse suit.

"Hey Chris, how ya feelin today?" Freddie asked with his usual enthusiasm.

"Great," I said, "Thanks for dinner last Friday. I appreciate it."

"Anytime. It was good catching up with you."

"Just checking to see if you made any progress with the software," I asked.

"You don't sound so good, you sure you're OK?"

I couldn't fool Freddie: I guess he could tell from my tone of voice I wasn't totally myself. "Yeah, just kind of battling with the demons, ya know?"

Fred laughed knowingly, "Yeah, I've been there. Why don't we hit the Palm Friday again and get some steaks – that'll cheer you up. It does wonders for me."

"I dunno know, I'm really tired. It's been a long week," I sighed.

Always the master salesman, Freddie wasn't taking no for an answer. "C'mon I'm buyin. Besides there's this dynamite waitress I want to introduce you to. She might even be the next Mrs. Blaire, ya never know."

I reluctantly agreed. I could tell he didn't want to discuss the software issue over the phone.

I got to the Palm a little late Friday night. Freddie was at the bar deep in conversation with a waitress who was obviously an aspiring actress; she just had that look about her. Freddie was in his element; he loved this stuff. He always looked the part of a movie star. That's what spending twenty years in the high-end garment industry will do to you, I guess.

"Hey Chris, glad you could make it. I want you to meet my new friend Katrina," he said.

I didn't want to meet anyone. Just wasn't in the mood, but I was trapped. With a forced smile I reached out and shook her hand, "Hi, nice to meet you."

"She's working her way onto Broadway and there is no way it's not gonna happen. You'll be seein her name in lights soon. I'm sure of it," Freddie said proudly.

Katrina smiled enthusiastically. "I hope so."

"She's gonna take care of us tonight. I got us the same table. I hope that's OK with you?"

"That's fine," I said.

We made our way to the back of the restaurant to our table. I was looking around for a clock of some sort because I didn't want to appear rude and be constantly checking my phone in front of Freddie while we were eating. But I needed to know that this wasn't going to last too long.

"Katrina's real nice, isn't she? She's a great kid; I hope things work out for her," Freddie said.

"Yeah she seems nice," I said flatly staring off into the abyss. "Any progress with Amir?"

"I'm working on some ideas. He's still not getting back to you, right?"

No, I haven't heard from him since our meeting."

"Give me a couple of days to think through what our next step is going to be. A buddy of mine from the VA is an attorney and I'm going to run some ideas past him about what he thinks we should do next," Freddie offered.

"Sounds good," I mumbled. I really didn't want to talk about it anyway; it just got more depressing the more I thought about it.

"How are things going with the business and your fiancée," he asked.

"Fighting the fight. Some days good, some bad. Mostly bad these days. It's déjà vu - everyday just seems the same – swimming in quicksand," I said.

"Wait till you get to my age, it's a speeding bullet. Every day I wake up, brush my teeth and ask myself, "Didn't this just happen a minute ago?" It's crazy how fast time seems to pass. It feels like yesterday I was in the jungles of Vietnam dodging bullets."

"Don't meet too many Vietnam Vets these days. You guys are becoming extinct. You said last time you did four tours, right?" I asked.

"Yeah, two on an aircraft carrier and two in the jungles," he said.

"How'd you ever get through that situation?"

"I fought it in the beginning. Didn't want to be there, but the powers that be, the U.S. government, decided my fate for me. I was resentful at my father for making me enlist. I was angry at the government for putting me in the war. I was angry at the Marine Corps. I hated being in that jungle. But I realized early on, the only way I was going to survive was if I accepted what was happening every day, the stark reality of my situation. I had to brutally accept what was happening to me, not how I wanted it to be."

He leaned over to me, "You have to adopt the same mindset with your life now. Your girl left you, the business is hemorrhaging money, this software thing is a nightmare – whatever you are going through. It seems you are not there yet mentally and emotionally."

"What do you mean?" I asked defensively.

"Not accepting the situation for what it is. You're still fighting and resisting the changes that are happening around you and to you."

"I don't know. I mean all these things are happening that's true; I just don't know how to manage them," I responded.

"Are you *really* accepting them for what they really are? Or are you wishing they were different?"

"Of course I wish they were different. I don't want to be dealing with this stuff," I replied.

"You think I wanted to deal with the war in the jungles of Vietnam? Getting shot at every day and having my best friends die around me? I hated every minute I was there, but I had to accept the situation all the way, completely and totally. You see, our minds are programmed to protect us from pain, and often create alternate realities to avoid or deny the reality in front of us," he explained.

"Denial?" I asked trying to defend myself.

"Denial is one defense mechanism. Fantasy and procrastination are others. A lot of people just complain about their lives and problems instead of taking action to rectify them. Your mind is pretty creative, you know; it'll find a way to block what it perceives as pain. In fact, one of its main jobs is to do exactly that. People often turn to drugs or alcohol to avoid the pain. I know I did. It's another common mechanism your mind uses.

"The way to cultivate acceptance – and it takes time, don't get me wrong – is to first write out on a piece of paper exactly what is happening and what you can or can't do about it. Wait; let me write this down for you so you can remember it later."

Freddie reached into his jacket pocket, pulled out a silver pen and started scribbling down on a napkin what he was saying.

"OK, the second thing is to notice what your attitude or perception is regarding the situation. What judgments are you making? For example, are you saying to yourself, 'She left me – this is horrible, or this is the end of my life? The business is tanking and there's nothing I can do about it?'

"Whatever your internal dialogue is telling you, write it down. Verbalize it. It takes away the power of the fear floating in your subconscious. When we verbalize it and write it down, it's easier to manage. We aren't just 'feeling' it and experiencing it hovering in our minds. It becomes somewhat tangible on paper. Don't make a judgment about it. The judgment about the situation only exacerbates the negative emotions and feelings. The situation just 'is.' Learn to cope with it head- on."

He paused for another sip. "Third, create an alternative response to the judgment that you repeat to yourself to counteract the negative responses you have allowed to develop. For instance, if you keep telling yourself 'She left me; this is the worst thing that has happened in my life,' change it to something like 'She left; it's out of my control; what is positive about this situation?' Flip it around and try to see it from a different point of view. You want to get your creative mind thinking in new and different directions.

"You know, Chris, we are literally programming our minds with fears and negative thoughts. You mentioned you were afraid about your financial future. Think about it. If you were to put your fear into a sentence, what would it say, 'I am afraid I am going to be destitute and homeless?' Something like that," Freddie asked.

"Yeah, something like that," I replied flatly.

"Write down your fear in a simple sentence and after it write the opposite in a positive format. For example, you are saying to yourself, 'I am afraid I am going to be destitute and homeless,' write out, 'I am feeling incredible joy at having financial abundance.' Or if you are thinking, 'I am afraid my fiancée is going to leave me,' you can write down, 'I am in love with the girl of my dreams.' Whatever it is, get your fear down on paper and write something more empowering. Focus on that new vision for your life.

"Fourth, start thinking of a new path for your life. Sometimes it's best to look at the worst- case scenario and work from there. When I was in Vietnam, the worst- case scenario in my mind was getting killed. Once I accepted that as a very real possibility, I found a deeper sense of peace about it. I wasn't as afraid; I wasn't thinking about it all the time. A strange calm came over me that seemed to melt away the fear of death. I started visualizing myself back in the States sitting on a beach enjoying the breeze of the ocean and the sun beaming down on me. I kept that picture in my mind everyday to get me through the rough spots.

"In your case, let's just say she leaves you for another guy. Accept that as a real possibility. What are you going to do? Life goes on. You can recreate your future. The key is not letting outside events dictate how we are going to feel internally about what is happening to us. We need to learn to center ourselves in the midst of the storm and create our own emotional stability as an anchor. Through a lot of personal struggles in my life I've learned how to do that." That's the power of acceptance.

Freddie slid the napkin across the table to me.

"Here's your homework assignment. Work through what I've written down and we'll meet again next Friday to go over your progress."

I looked at the napkin and across the top it read:

ACCEPT YOUR REALITY AS IT IS, NOT AS YOU WANT IT OR WISH IT TO BE.

Below were the four things he outlined for me to practice acceptance. I was a little taken aback by Freddie's forwardness, and giving me a homework assignment was a little presumptuous I thought. However, I figured I'd give it a shot.

Chapter Eleven

BRING LIGHT INTO SOMEONE'S DARKNESS

> As far as we can discern, the sole purpose of human existence is to kindle a light in the darkness of mere being.
>
> ~ *Carl Jung*

The following Friday arrived pretty quickly. We sat at the same table in the back at the Palm restaurant. I was not in the mood to deal with anything or anyone as usual, though Freddie's little homework assignment on acceptance was helping a little. I was having some shifts in my perception, but not enough. I wasn't even sure if I could manage talking with Freddie at this point. But he was buying and I was hungry.

"I hope you don't mind, but I've ordered already. I got the same as last week if that's OK with you?"

"That's fine. You were right; those are the best steaks in the city." I managed a grin.

"I told ya. How ya feeling today, Chris?" Freddie asked in his usual animated voice.

"Nothing's really changed since last Friday, Freddie, to be honest. Things just keep getting worse; it looks like we lost another account."

Freddie laughed with a sense of familiarity. "Yeah that sounds about right. Murphy's law, no?"

"I guess so," I said as I threw back another seltzer with lime. "It just seems to be getting harder and harder to manage…feeling it's getting bleaker."

Just as I was finishing my sentence the food arrived. My mood changed instantly. The scent of the sizzling steaks and fettuccine alfredo profoundly impacted my feeling. Funny how food can do that!

"Let me ask you, what are you doing to bring light into the darkness?" he asked inquisitively as he took a monstrous bite of his steak.

"What do you mean?"

"Chris, darkness and hardships will come into your life. They're inevitable. They will show up. I don't care who you are or how much money you have or don't have. The winter will follow the fall as certain as night follows day. It's part of nature, part of life. You should see it as such. Even in the universe the cosmic battle of light and darkness is literally happening as we speak. So you're making a judgment about what is happening to you and allowing it to influence your emotions," Freddie said calmly. "The darkness will get darker unless you fight against it. It's in your power to choose the light."

"I just don't know what to do. It's as if everything hit all at once. I can't seem to get out from under the weight of it all," I confessed.

"There are two ways to get out of the darkness," he pointed out. "One is to be the light to someone else, and the other is to allow someone to bring light into your life. Listen, at one point in my life I was rocketing to the top. I was living in Dallas, happily married with two kids, had a multimillion-dollar consulting apparel business, and owned a bunch of commercial buildings in and around Dallas worth millions of dollars. I thought I was bulletproof just as I had been in Vietnam.

"Then it all hit – like an earthquake. The ghosts of the past came back to torment me as I started experiencing the effects of Post-Traumatic Stress Disorder. Severe depression, nightmares, haunting visions plagued me incessantly and I didn't even know what was happening to me.

"I was becoming numb to reality and started drinking to shut off the pain. Here was I working eighteen hours a day to build my empire, to build the perfect life but it seemed to all happen overnight. A major recession hit Dallas and the real estate market collapsed, my marriage deteriorated, my wife filed for divorce, took the kids and left me. I couldn't maintain my apparel company, so I filed for bankruptcy. In a moment, I lost everything and fell into a deeper depression.

"I knew I couldn't stay in Texas choking on the smoldering ruins of what was once my life. After I signed the paperwork for divorce and filed for bankruptcy all within a few weeks of each other, I packed my bags and moved back to New York City to live with my brother Lloyd to rebuild my life. Our unconditional love for each other was the light I needed to save myself. He was the one person in my life I knew could help pull me out of my darkness.

"Once I got there, I asked myself over and over again: 'What is the next best step I can take right now?' And depressed as I was, I could only do the next step in front of me. The answer kept coming up: the next best step was to quit drinking. I knew if I kept drinking to numb the pain it would ultimately consume and destroy me. Lloyd had been sixteen years sober and convinced me to get involved in a twelve-step program with him. As hard as it was, I cleaned myself up and got to work on changing my life.

"I asked myself over and over again, "What is the next best step I can take right now?" Get a job! I had been a salesman my whole life, but couldn't get employment for the life of me, so I took a job as a stock clerk. Can you imagine, Chris? Just months before, I was worth over $20 million, and now I was working stocking shelves at a supermarket! I still had contacts in the apparel business and I worked my network until I finally got a job as a manufacturer's representative. I threw myself wholeheartedly into my new career, knowing full well what was at stake if I failed."

As usual, Freddie had a great story to relate to what I was going through, but it really wasn't helping. "That's an uplifting story, Freddie, and I appreciate it, but I don't see how that helps me with what I'm going through. It's not going to bring her back. It's not going to salvage the business," I lamented.

He was not offended. "I was alluding to the fact that you need someone to bring the light into your darkness, and it might not happen the way you expect it to. Your mission is to survive the darkness, and figure out a way out into the light to overcome the obstacle in your life. The reality is not everyone makes it out of their darkness. And it is their darkness. I can't judge your situation looking at it from the outside. It might not seem that bad to me, but you're feeling the pain and I'm not walking in your shoes. As your friend, I can only relate to you what I've experienced, what I've gone through and how I changed my life."

He faced me again, "Let me ask you, Chris, what are you good at? Computers?"

"I guess so," I said weakly. I wasn't sure where he was going with this line of questioning but I let him run with it.

"Why don't you volunteer teaching computers to underprivileged kids or something like that? Go down to the Bowery and teach computers to some of the guys in the shelter. Step outside your chaos and put yourself in the light," Freddie offered.

"Are you serious?" I wasn't sure if he was joking or not.

"I'm dead serious," said Freddie. "You've worked on Wall Street, you get the concept of return on investment, right? Think of this project as a spiritual investment, in other words, a karmic investment. You're investing your time, energy and effort into helping others with no expectation of return, but the reality is there is always, a return on your investment. By bringing light into another person's world, you actually illuminate your own. You will actually be solving your own darkness problem," Freddie explained.

"Volunteer at a homeless shelter teaching computers? That's your answer, your solution to what's going on in my life?" I asked again, just to make sure we were on the same wavelength. "I can barely get out of bed every day and you're asking me to go to a homeless shelter and teach total strangers computer skills. Right?"

There was a long pause at the table as Freddie finished another bite of his steak. He pulled out his silver pen and wrote across the top of his napkin:

LIVE YOUR LIFE REACHING DOWN WITH ONE HAND TO PULL SOMEONE UP AND REACHING UP WITH THE OTHER HAND ASKING FOR HELP FOR SOMEONE TO PULL YOU UP ALL THE WHILE LOOKING UP TO HIGHER AND BETTER WAYS.

"Always ask yourself: What is the next best step? The next best step to bring light into your life is to bring light to someone else." He smiled as he slid the napkin across the table. "Besides, Chris, like I always ask you, what's the worst that could happen? You change someone's life for the better? Sounds like a pretty good deal to me."

It was hard to argue with Freddie's logic as I contemplated his suggestion. If his advice was as good as his food choices, I knew I was making the right decision.

Chapter Twelve

LISTEN TO THE UNIVERSE

We must accept finite disappointment, but never lose infinite hope.

~ *Martin Luther King Jr.*

Freddie suggested we mix it up Friday night and meet at the Polo Club on 55th Street. I had never been there, so I figured, why not? I arrived a little late and weaved my way through the crowd, noticing a few celebrities along the way, and took a seat across from Freddie. I could tell Freddie was genuinely glad to be alive. It wasn't an act. He was truly grateful to be in this present moment in time and was taking it in for what it was. I wasn't as enamored, but I pretended to seem interested. "Isn't this place great?" Freddie exclaimed as he looked around the restaurant in awe like a five-year-old kid at his first day at a baseball stadium. The Polo Club was owned by Ralph Lauren and the ambience radiated his sophistication throughout the building. It was decorated with deep mahogany colored furniture and meticulously stained wood panels adorned with everything polo related – pictures of majestic horses, mallets, polo helmets, you name it. I felt like I was in a Conde' Nast ad.

"Yeah, it's pretty cool," I said, as I nursed my new favorite drink: seltzer water with a twist of lime.

"I ordered the seafood platter for both of us – it's the best in the city," he said. Freddie had been a salesman in New York City for years and knew all the great spots.

I still wasn't sure why I had agreed to meet with Freddie every Friday. Maybe I was hoping he would help me get some answers to what was plaguing my life. Maybe I needed to be distracted for a few hours from obsessing over my own problems. Either way, the food was always amazing; I couldn't deny that, and I always felt better after we met. I must admit I enjoyed Freddie's company. He had an energy about him that radiated goodness, and his stories were always very entertaining.

"What's new in your world, Chris? You volunteerin or what?" he asked me. I noticed the New Yorker in Freddie sneak out when he was in his element.

"I did, actually. I went down to the Bowery Mission and met with the project coordinator and we talked about setting up a little computer network there where I could teach the guys. He was open to it and said he was going to get back to me soon. "So we're making some progress," I reported.

"How did it feel?" he asked.

"I dunno how I feel about anything anymore, but...next best step, right?"

"Now you're gettin it," said Freddie with a broad grin.

"Did you have a chance to speak with Amir?" I asked, not sure if I even wanted an answer.

"I spoke with my friend the attorney and showed him the contract you have with Amir. Basically, he told me that by the time you get everything done through the lawyers and all that nonsense, you'll wind up spending more than you put into it, so it's not worth it. Nobody ever wins in those situations except the lawyers. Is Amir getting back to you at all?" Freddie asked, although I'm sure he already knew the answer.

“Nothing. No emails no phone calls,” I moaned.

“Well, if he won’t come to us we should go to him. Do you know where he lives?”

“Yeah, of course, I’ve been to his house in Queens a few times. Why? ”

“I’m gonna stop by, pay him a visit. See if I can meet him on his home turf and get an answer from him on what’s going on with the project and the money,” Freddie said decisively.

“If you want to go. Whatever works at this point…I don’t know what else to do.” “Yeah, I think that’s a good plan. Send me his address later and I’ll stop by his house during the week.”

“You got it,” I told him.

“How are things with your fiancée?” he asked.

“Not good, kind of the same story. She gets back to me when she feels like it, which is sporadic at best, so it’s difficult to coordinate with her. The business continues to bleed money and I’m not exactly setting the world on fire running it here. I just don’t see it getting any better, honestly, Freddie,” I admitted.

Freddie paused. “Did you ever hear the story of the farmer, his son and the horse?”

“No.”

“Well, there was this farmer and he was poor, very poor. He only had one horse to help him farm his land. Then one day his one and only horse escaped from the barn and vanished into the forest. His neighbor came by to lament the farmer’s misfortune.

‘I’m so sorry to hear what happened to your horse – that’s just bad luck,’ said the neighbor.

The farmer stared into the distance, ‘Maybe it’s bad, maybe it’s good. Time will tell.’

The next day the horse that escaped came back to the barn with another horse. The neighbor saw the horse with his new friend and went back to visit the farmer. ‘What good luck! Your horse came back with another one!’ he said.

‘Maybe it’s good luck. Maybe it’s bad luck. Time will tell,’ the farmer replied.

The next day the farmer's son was riding on the new horse and fell off and broke his leg. The neighbor ran out to help him. 'What terrible luck! Your son has a broken leg!' the neighbor lamented.

The farmer remained stoic. 'Maybe it's bad, maybe it's good. Time will tell.'

The next day a group of soldiers visited the farmer. There was a war going on, a draft for young men was enacted and the farmer's son was of age to be drafted. When the leader of the soldiers realized that the farmer's son wasn't eligible to serve in the army because of his broken leg, they left the farm.

Again, the neighbor came to visit the farmer. 'What good luck! Your son isn't able to serve in the military, so his life is spared!' he said.

'Maybe it's good luck, maybe it's bad. Time will tell,' said the farmer."

Freddie took a breath. "It goes on like that, but you see the point I am trying to make, Chris. What you see as a terrible situation in your life, might actually be a blessing in disguise. Time will tell."

"I understand what you're getting at, but I can't see how anything in my life is going to get better at all."

"That's the whole point! You can't see it now. When the farmer had a catastrophic event happen in his life, he took on a detached indifferent attitude towards the event. He chose his response. That's what you gotta do... choose. Choose your emotional response to everything around you. Choose not to worry about the future but have faith that it's going to be better than you could ever imagine. Choose to see the beauty and gratitude in your life now, despite your situation."

He reached into his jacket pocket and pulled out a small intricate jade buddha statue and held it up to the light. "Hey, check this out. I got this from a kid in a village on the river in Vietnam," he said as he handed it to me.

I looked it over with intense interest. "Wow, unbelievable detail!" I commented with admiration. "This is a Buddha?"

"Yeah, our platoon stopped at a local village along the Mekong Delta. We were all exhausted having not slept for almost two days straight, so we decided to get a diversion from the monotony of the river. We tried to stay on the boat as much as possible. It was just too dangerous to get off because we could get ambushed at any moment; but sometimes we took a chance and pulled over. It was a gamble, but when you're stuck on a boat twelve feet long with four other guys, you need a change of scenery now and then. I could almost 'feel' if a village was dangerous, and this one had a calm effect to it."

"I can't imagine living like that – so scary," I said as I handed the figurine back to Freddie. He held it with a sense of religious reverence.

"I got this a couple of days right after my best friend on the riverboat was shot and killed. I was at the lowest ebb of my life. Nothing had any meaning anymore. I didn't want to live and thought I was going to die on the river in the middle of nowhere.

"I pulled the boat off the river to barter a little with some of the locals and a flurry of children came running to meet us – which wasn't uncommon. The innocence and excitement of the kids were bright light in my darkness. There was no war with them. No depression. No enmity. Just strangers meeting strangers and the common bond of humanity between us.

"One little boy ran up to me holding up this little Buddha statue. The smile on his face brought back a glimmer of hope to my soul that things were going to be OK. I always carried around a bunch of candies with me and they usually went a long way when bartering with the locals. We made the trade and the look in his eyes and the smile on his face gave me a renewed sense of hope that my humanity wasn't lost.

"I was in the darkest days of my life, but look, here we are now enjoying the best lobsters New York City has to offer! You just never know what is around the next bend in the river of your life, Chris," Freddie said glowingly as he admired the Buddha figurine. "Have you heard the phrase 'God is in the pause'?" he asked.

"No," I replied.

"I learned this from a buddy of mine in Vietnam. He would stop three or four times a day, close his eyes and just listen and center his mind. A form of mediation, I guess. He taught me how to do it and it changed my life." Freddie brought out the silver pen, grabbed a napkin and started scribbling away.

"Here's what you do: Close your eyes and just count your breath for fifteen to twenty times just to focus your thinking. Center your mind on what you're hearing around you – the noises, the sounds. Notice the smells. Feel the sensations in your body. Allow your mind to experience the moment from a sensory perspective. Slow your breathing and just focus on the physical sensations happening to you. Maybe your arm starts to itch. Don't react; just tell yourself, 'I am acknowledging my arm itches in this moment.'

"Close your eyes and listen to the sounds around you. Listen to the Universe. Quiet your mind briefly and listen to the world. Learn to appreciate it and your time here on it. Allow your brain to soak in the gratitude and wonder of life.

"Do that for a few moments, just allowing your mind to acknowledge what is happening in the moment. No judgment. Next, think about what's great in your life, who loves you, who you love, great moments you've had, and moments you want to have.

"Finally, get a picture of what and where you want to go and who you want to be. This takes practice. You have to cultivate this positive future. You are so stuck in your present circumstances and the negativity surrounding them that your mind is completely focused on what is wrong and how bad things are. Gotta give it a new image. It's like changing the channel on your TV. It will help shift your mind away from your present focus on what you are perceiving and what you don't have.

"I started doing this in Vietnam and still do it to this day to help quiet my mind and center my emotions. The key is to create within your imagination a better vision of your future, and to keep it constantly in front of you."

"I guess I could try it," I said somewhat skeptically.

He slid the napkin across the table.

"Hey, like I always say, nothing ventured nothing gained. Besides, what's the worst that could happen?"

I was beginning to see how Freddie was trying to teach and pass on to me what he'd learned in his life. I picked up the napkin and looked over what Freddie had written.

"Three times a day?" I asked.

"The more the better, but do it at least three times a day. Try doing it before you eat anything. It's easy to remember it that way. Like praying in a way, a form of thanksgiving," he explained.

Freddie took one last admiring look at the figurine. He reached across the table and extended the Buddha statue to me. "I want you to have this, Chris," he said.

"I can't take this, Freddie," I said.

"I want you to have it, Chris." He extended it to me emphatically.

"Here's your glimmer of hope for your future," he said with a gleam in his eye. "Keep it near you. When you wake up and go to bed brushing your teeth, give thanks for another day on the planet. It's a magical world we live in. You're just going through a hard time now but, as I always tell you, just remember...nothing lasts forever. The light returns, the storm subsides, the wind blows over and the war ends," he said calmly.

I knew what the small statue of Buddha meant to Freddie and the significance it held in his life. Here was a total stranger giving me a tangible piece of hope – literally. I was starting to believe there was a better way for me and for some strange reason the Universe had brought Freddie into my life to help guide me onto that new path.

Chapter Thirteen

STAY IN THE MOMENT

Some of us think holding on makes us strong but sometimes it is letting go.

~ *Hermann Hesse*

I met up with Freddie at the Polo Club again. I was craving their garlic mashed potatoes from the last time we met. Some things in life are worth doing twice. I got there before him and made a few phone calls, so I didn't feel foolish sitting there alone with nothing and no one around me. What did people do before cell phones to look busy? I guess I'd be reading a book or pretending to be writing something important.

When he arrived, I noticed he wasn't in his usual good spirits.

"What's the matter? You seem down."

Freddie paused. I could tell he was thinking of what to say to me, or if he should say anything at all. "My oldest daughter got arrested again."

"For what?" I asked, not exactly sure I wanted to know.

"She's been struggling with mental illness and heroin addiction for quite a few years now and she got picked up on a charge yesterday. It breaks my heart, Chris, to see her like that. As her father, there is nothing I can do at this point. She's a grown woman and makes her own decisions," he said helplessly.

I didn't know what to say so I sat in silence waiting for Freddie to keep the conversation going. It seemed like hours before he started back up again.

"What do you do with that, Chris? Let it go. Give it to God. Let her work out her own karma with the Universe and pray she gets her life back? All I can do is be there for her the best I know how. When you›re raising your kids you think only the best things are going to happen and somehow as a parent you can guide them around the landmines of life...but things unfold the way they do."

I wasn't used to seeing Freddie like this. I was wishing I could dive back into my phone and hide in my world of pretend and illusion. Reality was difficult to deal with and I was an expert at avoiding it; yet here it was right in front of Freddie and he was taking it head-on.

"And I thought raising a puppy was difficult," I replied awkwardly with an equally awkward laugh trying not to pick up Freddie's spirit. Freddie forced a smile.

"She was a great kid up until around eighth grade when she started having problems with depression and got into drugs. It's been a struggle ever since then. Her mother and I have tried for years to help her: a bunch of rehabs, therapy, everything. It's all the same process though, Chris, decisions we made, things we didn't do or did, all these things have ramifications that reverberate through the rest of our lives. We're going to make mistakes – it's inevitable, we're human. It's part of the process. We have to live with the consequences. Like everything in life, it's how we respond to what is happening to us and around us."

As we were talking, I saw the waitress walking towards us with our food. Out of nowhere someone accidentally bumped into her and I watched as my beloved garlic potatoes went flying through the air crashing to the floor getting ground under the feet of patrons in the restaurant who were oblivious of my disaster.

"Damn there goes our food! I'm starving!" I shouted.

Freddie threw me a smile. "See what I mean, Chris – we are powerless over so many things in life. Gotta let it go. What can you do? The food is now on the floor instead of our table. What are you going to do?" Freddie asked.

"Nothing I can do. Wait for the replacement, I guess," I said shrugging my shoulders.

"All you really can do at this point. On the other hand, you can choose your response instead of reacting and getting angry or upset or whatever emotional response pops up. I choose to patiently wait for the next round," he said.

"It's easy to do that with a plate of food, Freddie. But I'm having a much harder time letting go of what's happening with my fiancée. She's not getting back to me; she won't answer my calls. I don't know what to do – it's eating me up inside," I complained as I watched the waitress clean up the mess.

"It reminds me of a story my mother used to tell me as a child when I would worry about something going on in my life. There was once an old Buddhist monk who was very fond of an ancient vase in the monastery where he lived. The vase had been there for centuries and he would often pass by daily and admire it for its craftsmanship and artistry. Every day he would pick a rose and place one inside it. One day, a junior monk was walking with him and noticed the abbot's fondness for the vase.

"'Why are you so attached to the vase? You of all people know that everything is temporary; we are living in a constant state of flux and impermanence. As surely as we sit here and the sun is beaming off the vase, it will be broken and shattered into a thousand pieces and will be no more. Are you not being untrue to your very teachings?' quizzed the junior monk.

"The abbot smiled knowingly. 'You see this rose bloom in all its glory?' he asked as he gently touched the petals of the rose.

'Of course,' replied the junior monk. 'We marvel at its beauty, its majesty. But for a brief moment it is here and gone.'

'In the same way, I know the vase is already gone; it's already broken and is no longer a vase. Similar to the rose, I admire its majesty for every moment I have with it, knowing it is already gone. What a precious gift we have been given!'

"Chris, it's like you're worrying about the vase being broken... it is guaranteed to be broken. Ultimately, I don't care if you're the richest man on the planet or the poorest. In the end, as with you and as with me, everything will be gone. You will let go of everything on *that day*," said Freddie with finality.

"Or life lets go of us," I added.

"That's another way of looking at," Freddie laughed. "When you adopt the idea that it's all impermanent and we are constantly moving in and out of events, moments, circumstances ...letting go isn't that difficult. We just hold on too long to the illusion that things are going to last. They don't.

"The reality of life is that we have very little control over so many things. Control is very much an illusion," he reminded me. A look came across his face as he stared into the distance. I could tell he was reflecting on the past events of his life.

"I realized early on in Vietnam that almost everything – and I mean everything there – was out of my control. I was the captain of the boat and all I had to control were the gas pedal and steering wheel, and many times those didn't even work the way I wanted them to. But I didn't control the current, I didn't control the wind, the enemy, the darkness – nothing.

"I asked myself, 'What do I have control over in this situation? What is out of my control? What actions can I take to influence this situation? What is the most effective attitude and perspective I can take to maintain emotional equilibrium?' I did all that subconsciously then. Now I do it on paper with everything in my life. It's easier to process it when I can see it, instead of when the feelings or emotions are just floating in my head."

He pulled his silver pen out of his pocket, grabbed a napkin from the table and started writing.

"Here we go again I thought...more napkin homework!"

Across the top of the napkin there were five columns. It read:

SITUATION	CONTROL	NO CONTROL	CREATIVE ACTION	ATTITUDE
My daughter got arrested; she is addicted to heroin.	Talk to her, give her advice, bring her to the doctor for help.	What she does, when she does it, with who she does it	Pray for her, talk to her, introduce her to friends who overcame their addictions. Bring her to skid row or the morgue to scare her sober.	Nonjudgmental. She is free to make her own choices; forgive her, forgive myself, unconditional love, let her go; she is in God's hands.

"Write down your situation...your fiancée is breaking up with you," he points to the napkin.

"She's not breaking up with me, Freddie," I retorted.

"If you say so, Chris, but from my vantage point that's what it looks like is going on. But it's your life. So what is the situation?" he asked.

"She is ignoring me," I said.

"What *do* you have control over?"

"Not much. I keep sending emails and calling her but she is not getting back to me."

"OK, so write down under the control column 'communicating with her.' What *don't* you have control over?" he asked.

"What she does or doesn't do. Like your daughter, she is going to make her own decisions. There is nothing else I can do at this point to get her attention," I told him.

"Write it down. Under creative actions write down what you've been doing, as well as something that you could do that would be, let's say, out of left field. You could send her a telegram, maybe have one of her friends call her on your behalf; you could fly out there. Think outside the box," he advised.

"Now, what about your attitude towards the situation? Not what it is now, but what it should be. What is the optimal most effective perspective on your situation?" he asked.

I had to stop and think about what I was already feeling – anger, hurt, frustration, confusion. I had to try and emotionally circumvent my feelings to find a more resourceful state of mind.

"I guess like you did: just letting go, being grateful for the time we had together, assuming it's over and thinking about moving on if she doesn't want to work it out," I concluded.

"Now you're making progress, Chris! Sit with this exercise for a few days and kind of think over what it is telling you as you allow your attitude to transition away from the negative feelings into the new mindset you are trying to create," he assured me. .

"Just ask yourself two things when you start drifting into worry or remorse: 'Where are my feet right now?' I'm here with you now, in the Polo Club, in the greatest city in the world, about to have an incredible dinner with a good friend. Everything else going on in my head is fiction – the worry, the fear, the remorse – all of it. It is a story you are telling and selling to yourself and it isn't even true.

"Then ask yourself, "What is great in my life...right now?" We're breathing, we have enough money to enjoy this dinner, and we're not stuck in some god-forsaken jungle in the middle of nowhere with bullets flying by our heads!" He raised his glass and we made a toast.

"I know plenty of guys who never made it out of Vietnam physically and emotionally, and who would love to be sitting where you are, where I am," Freddie said with a certain sadness.

As we were toasting the waitress circled back to our table with our food. "Sorry for the delay, guys; these are on the house," she said as she slid us both a slice of apple pie next to our dinner. Freddie sat up in his seat and we both thanked her profusely for her generosity.

"See how that works out, Chris? You were getting angry and upset about the food and, voilà, two wonderful pieces of apple pie on the house. If you hadn't changed your attitude and perspective when it happened, if you hadn't let it go, the last half hour of your life would have been spent being angry and upset. Instead, you spent it patiently waiting, enjoying our conversation and you got rewarded with a slice of apple pie.

"The question now is: are you ready to change your life?"

I just kept on eating. I was definitely not ready to answer that question right now. That would have to wait until next Friday.

Chapter Fourteen

RETREAT INTO NATURE

Always be yourself, express yourself, have faith in yourself.

~ *Bruce Lee*

That Friday morning I was exhausted. I had a brutal week and today wasn't getting any better. There was no way I was going to make it to the restaurant tonight to see Freddie. It was going to be an "under-the-covers hide-from-the-world" night, so I texted Freddie and canceled our meeting. Texting was such a great way to avoid conflict and contact. But Freddie wasn't going to let me off the hook that easily. He called me right after the text and convinced me to meet up with him at my office which was across the street from my apartment, so I didn't have to travel. He said he was bringing the best Chinese food in New York City, and as much as I tried, I couldn't talk my way out of it. Freddie was too good of a salesman.

7:00 pm sharp Freddie was right on time at my office. We made our way to the conference room to drop off the food. Freddie looked around my office with the same childlike curiosity he had in the restaurant.

"You got a great setup here, Chris; you should be proud of what you've accomplished. Why don't you give me the nickel tour?" he asked.

"Let's go," I replied, trying to match his enthusiasm.

"Oh – before I forget – I made a little visit to Amir's house the other day. Quite an interesting meeting!" he exclaimed.

That was news. "What happened?"

"Well, he wasn't home, but I had a very lovely conversation with his wife Thelma. A very nice lady, I might add. We spoke for almost half an hour, and it seems like your buddy Amir is in the middle of a nasty divorce and that probably would explain what is going on with the money. His wife told me Amir is living with his brother in Brooklyn and she gave me the address there. I'll stop by later in the week and have a conversation with him about the next steps regarding the software," he explained.

"Sounds like a plan," I said. I was glad Freddie was handling the software situation; I just didn't have the energy to deal with it.

As we walked around the office, Freddie started firing away with the questions: "How many employees do you have right now? How long have you been in the business? What are the main services and products you are providing? What are the most profitable sectors you sell to? Who are your major competitors? What is your competitive angle, your unique selling position?"

Frankly speaking, I just wasn't in the mood to talk shop about the company. "It doesn't matter, Freddie, because it's all slipping away. Twelve years of blood, sweat and tears and I'm watching it all spill down the drain in front of my eyes."

"Why do you denigrate what you've accomplished here?" he interrupted. You've built something impressive – don't discount it."

"The thing that bothers me most is I'm starting not to care. Doesn't seem to have any meaning anymore. I built this with my fiancée and she's gone now."

"It doesn't have meaning or the meaning has changed?" he asked.

"Both."

I continued with the tour and Freddie continued firing the questions. We headed back to the conference room and sat down to eat. Freddie was right again about his food choices – this was the best Chinese food I had ever eaten in New York. He continued with the cross- examination as I struggled with the chopsticks.

Hey Freddie, do you have any forks in that bag?" I asked.

He laughed as he passed me a fork, while he manipulated his chopsticks with the grace of an orchestra conductor.

"What is your favorite part of the business? What do you like to do within the company?" Freddie continued with the questions.

"Starting the company, collaborating with my fiancée, developing the content, and building the website, that kind of stuff," I said.

"So you like creating? That seems to be in your nature. That is who you are. It's not like you're standing around running calculations on excel spreadsheets and crunching numbers, right?"

"No, I hate that stuff," I replied.

"Do you enjoy dealing with the customers, the employees, and account receivables? The real day-to-day stuff of the business?" Freddie asked again.

"Not really, no. In fact, it's like torture especially when I'm depressed, which is almost all the time. I just want to be alone," I told him.

"It doesn't seem like you want to run a business and be with this girl anymore, so

why are you still here?" Freddie asked pointedly.

"I'm making good money," I responded matter-of-factly.

"Who told you this is what you should be doing with your life, Chris?" he

persisted.

"I dunno. My father was in business and it seemed like the best way to make money.

And I built this with my fiancée," I reasoned.

"So you're doing this because your father did it, and for money and with your ex-

fiancée who is now living in Switzerland?" he asked.

"More or less; those are most of the reasons, I guess, yes. Gotta make a living somehow, right?" I said.

"There's a million ways to make a living. Society tells us you should be rich, or look like this, or you should drive a certain car, or have a certain status that *they* have established," Freddie responded. "What you should do is strive to be happy! You only get one shot at the title, Chris. Don't waste your time living an unfulfilled life. Why not do what your soul is telling you to do?"

"Soul? I have no idea what you are talking about," I told him.

"Well, let me ask you, what do you like doing when you're not doing this? Ya know, in your free time on Saturday?"

"Sleeping! It's my favorite habit. If they could pay me to sleep I would be a millionaire," I joked.

Freddie laughed at my feeble attempt at humor. He grabbed a pair of chopsticks on the table and broke off one and started waving it in the air at me.

"Let me give you the magic wand test," he smiled as he continued waving the chopstick at me like some insane wizard.

"What's that?" I asked.

"If I could wave a magic wand over your life, what would you do if you had all the money you needed? Who would you be?" he inquired. I started to see where he was going with this.

"How much are we talking about?" I asked him.

"Nothing ridiculous. You're not Jeff Bezos or Mick Jagger – not saying you can't be, but let's say with all your needs met, you don't have to worry about money. You're good. You're comfortable."

"I would probably live on some beach somewhere writing screenplays or books all day, enjoying my life, in love with the woman of my dreams, and be happy no matter what," I mused.

"So you're a writer?" Fred asked.

"I wouldn't say I'm a writer. I write things, sort of as a hobby. Helps me forget about my life for a while. Escape to another world that I can create in my mind."

"What have you written?" he asked curiously.

"Finishing up a screenplay and halfway through my first novel," I told him.

"You *are* a writer, Chris. You are a creator. I don't write anything, ever. I can barely spell my own name," said Freddie laughing. "What if you could get paid for writing? Make what you're making now but for writing, not running a business with your ex-fiancée. Would you do it?" Freddie asked me.

"In a heartbeat, I'd do it now and no one pays me," I said.

"There you go!" Freddie said as he flicked the imaginary wand toward me as if he was Harry Potter casting a spell. He turned the magic wand back into one of his chopsticks and scarfed down a mound of Lo Mein.

"What are you talking about?" I asked him.

"We just figured out what should be your goal. Sounds like that is your dream. You

should be working toward that picture in your mind," he remarked.

"Yeah that all sounds great. But I got this business here and what you're talking about is ridiculous. I can't just pick up and leave," I protested.

"Someone's making a living writing, so why not you?"

"I dunno; it's really difficult. Besides, I've got a multimillion-dollar business here, an office and an apartment on Wall Street. Not to mention the fact that I'm supposed to be getting married...well, maybe," I replied weakly.

"Yeah...and...you're miserable. I'm talking to you as your friend, Chris. You can lie to yourself that you have this and that and a business etc. I'm not buying it. By the way, I'm not saying you have to be a writer or should be; I'm just saying, get in touch with your true self and make decisions about your life from that place," Freddie told me.

"You make it so easy to just change my life. It's not as simple, Freddie, as waving a

magic chopstick around," I told him.

"I'm not saying it's going to be easy; I'm just saying it's worth doing. It takes effort and energy to align your soul with your authentic self, but once you do, your divine path will take you like a current to your destiny. You will no longer be achieving to be happy. You will be happy regardless of external circumstances as you achieve, as your life unfolds along its journey.

"Think about children; they aren't trying to be anything other than who they are. They are completely and always true to their authentic selves. It's in the process of living that children unlearn and detach from their true selves and get programmed by society, family and other outside sources. We have to relearn and reconnect to that part of ourselves which is in us, our soul or spirit, whatever you want to call it. It doesn't happen overnight, but I've found the best way to start this process is getting away for a time from your current life, being alone with yourself and getting back to nature," he said.

"Like join an ashram or a kibbutz?" I said sarcastically. We both laughed.

"You can do that if you want, but there's an easier way. The best way I've found is to get away from your environment completely. No cellphone, no email, no TV, no radio, no internet, definitely no New York City and definitely no Central Park. The less people generally, the better. Just you and the Universe. Spend two days in nature away from traffic, chaos and noise – anything that clouds your mind," he advised.

"You're serious? So what, go rent a cabin in the woods or something?" I asked half-jokingly.

"You can if you want. The key is to get out into nature – could be the ocean, forest, go on a hike in the mountains," he explained. He pulled out his famous silver pen, grabbed a napkin and started writing. I knew I was in for some heavy homework.

"And what may I ask am I going to do for two days? I'm going to be bored out of my mind."

"That's part of the process. You're not bored now; you're distracted by the 'noise' of this life you are in. The idea is to step outside your current life, if only for a couple of days, to connect and observe yourself living. Alone, with a mission to listen, appreciate, write, see and create a new life in your imagination. Write the new and next chapter of your life. When you step outside the rhythms of your own life and into the rhythms of nature, it changes your awareness. It's healing and will help guide you into your soul's true path," Freddie told me with a smile. "Oh, and bring a pen and notebook. That's key," he added casually.

"A pen and notebook? What are those?" I said jokingly. "Haven't used either of them in probably ten years. Can I bring my laptop?" I asked.

"No, definitely not" Freddie said emphatically. "That's part of the problem: we've allowed technology to rule our lives. We can't and don't go anywhere without it. There is a very different experience within your brain, putting pen to paper. The act of formulating a thought and your own hand writing it down on paper has a much more powerful impact on your subconscious mind," he explained.

"You're going to be writing…a lot. I want you to be completely detached and open minded. Whatever you hear and feel, write down everything - no judgment when thoughts come into your mind, though. Never question your thoughts. Practice the silent pauses – listen to the world, listen to your soul speaking to you. Thoughts are going to be swirling in your mind – worry, fear, fiancée, money, joy, confusion – whatever comes to mind, write it down...ideas, memories, desires whatever," he instructed.

"Next, write at the top of one page:

WHAT AM I GRATEFUL FOR IN MY LIFE

"Start brainstorming. Whatever comes to mind, start writing – your ability to see, taste, breathe the ocean air, friends you have, family, great moments in your life, whatever comes into consciousness. When you get your mind in a state of complete gratitude and you focus on what is great in your life, the thoughts your imagination starts to manufacture will be much more in tune with creating a better future life for you.

"Next write at the top of another page:

MY PERFECT DAY

"Where are you? Who are you with? What are your feelings? What are you experiencing? What are you doing for work? All too often we get stuck in fear, worry and anxiety, which are all based on future images and feelings we create in our minds within our imaginations. It's all fiction. That's all fear and worry really are – made-up stories we tell ourselves and believe are true and going to happen. We need to train our imaginations to create positive and empowering images and feelings for our future. You're creating that future in your mind, and when you write it down you can constantly reference it and go back to it. As you think about it, more and more will it become part of your subconscious mind and start pulling you in the direction of your authentic self. That's why I want you to write your perfect day.

"It doesn't make sense how all this is going to help me in my predicament?" I told him.

He continued without conceding to me. "If we merely listened to our intellect, we'd never fall in love; we would never create art; music would be irrelevant. I'm just asking you to suspend judgment for a weekend. Besides, like I asked you before, "What's the worst that could happen? What have you got to lose? A weekend away from the city?"

"Yeah, I guess you're right," I surrendered.

He didn't miss a beat and dived right into the next homework assignment. "Finally, write down on another sheet of paper at the top:

HOW CAN I BE OF SERVICE TO MY FELLOW MAN?

"Ask yourself this question daily, constantly. Brainstorm ways you could be helpful to others, things you can do to bring goodness to the people around you. You don't necessarily have to save the world, but you can if you decide to. Start thinking of ways to serve the world. Remember what Albert Einstein once said, 'Only a life lived in the service of others is worth living,'" he said encouragingly.

"OK, so I ***am*** going to an ashram; it's just for a weekend and it's in the woods?" I summed it up sarcastically.

"Pretty much," Fred laughed, not minding my remark. "You won't be alone though. Just consider yourself going on a retreat with nature, God, and your soul. I promise it's going to be an amazing experience!" He reached across the table and opened up a container of fried rice.

"How's the volunteering going by the way?" he asked.

"I start next week. Got the books on order and will be meeting at The Bowery Mission once a week for two hours. Looks like we are going to have three or four guys in the class. I'm bringing over some old computers...we'll see where it goes."

"Now you're taking a step towards connecting with your authentic self." He smiled wisely as he devoured another bite of Lo Mein sprinkled with fried rice and slid the napkin with my homework assignment across the table.

Chapter Fifteen

CONFRONT YOUR FEARS

> You gain strength, courage and confidence by every experience in which you really stop to look fear in the face. You are able to say to yourself, "I have lived through this horror. I can take the next thing that comes along." You must do the thing you think you cannot do.
>
> *~Eleanor Roosevelt*

It was the fall of 2008 and fear hung in the air like smog over the nation. It was particularly thick on Wall Street where I was living and working. The stock market was melting in front of our eyes. Rumors of the next Great Depression were starting to swirl. No one in my generation had seen anything even remotely similar to what was happening, except perhaps for the 9/11 attacks. People were losing their jobs left and right and no one was sure when it would end – if it would end. Scary times!

Freddie invited me to his apartment on Friday for a home cooked dinner with his wife and told me to bring my notebook. I always looked forward to my Friday meetings with Freddie; they were a welcome break from the drama that was my life. When I arrived at Freddie's apartment, the food was already laid out across the table like a Thanksgiving feast. The apartment was modestly decorated. A shrine to Freddie's career in the Military decorated an entire wall. Photos of the war, friends lost, ribbons, medals. He had lived another life in those four years. Another shrine – I would actually call it a temple – lined the opposite wall. All of Freddie's sacred books and texts were arranged in sections according to Freddie's interests. There had to be thousands of books; all of them had an outward "wear" to them. I'm sure Freddie had ingested them thoroughly with all his trademark zeal. I was starting to understand where Freddie's wisdom came from.

Before I could break the awkward silence I felt and comment on Freddie's prolific library, his wonderful wife Jane took me by the arm and brought me to my seat at the table. She was Freddie's better half I could tell. Jane had such a kind, warm and loving energy that made me feel like I was part of their family.

"Wow, what a spread, Jane! Thanks for inviting me over!" I complimented Freddie's wife as the aroma from the brisket took a hold of my senses. I was feeling a little inadequate for only bringing a frozen banana cream pie from Walmart.

"Let's dig in," Freddie shouted as he carved up the brisket and passed pieces around the table. He and his wife quietly paused before taking a bite, so I joined in the silence. It was a great moment to be alive in spite of the insanity happening in the world around us.

"I saw the stock market was down again today 500 points," I said trying to break the awkward silence at the table.

"Well, won't be the first time and won't be the last. What goes up comes down. Right, isn't that what they say?" Freddie commented unaffected.

"I guess so. It's just scary to watch your money disappear in front of your eyes. I'm having trouble sleeping," I said trying to hide the fear underneath.

"What's so scary about it? Gonna lose all that money...and?" Freddie asked me.

"I worked hard for that money. I don't want to lose it," I told him alluding to the obvious.

"Gives you a sense of security?" Freddie asked.

"Absolutely!" I replied.

"Yeah, that's a horrifying feeling when that sense of security is stripped from you. All you've known, all the comfort of society we've built to insulate us, is gone. Let me tell you about losing everything," Freddie said.

"Oh, here we go!" said Jane.

Freddie laughed. "She's heard this a million times, but it's worth repeating to you, Chris. I'll never forget my first day driving a swift boat up the Mekong Delta. Everything American was gone. I was living on a twelve-foot boat, with four boat mates, a lot of ammo and a little food. Everything I valued in my life was gone. My life in Hawaii, my best friend who died on the boat trying to save me, the girl I was going to marry, my country – everything. Add to that driving aimlessly in the dark jungles of Vietnam, getting shot at constantly, attacked by mosquitoes relentlessly, snakes and every other horror you could imagine. Now that's fear!" Freddie exclaimed.

"Oh, the snakes would be horrible!" cried Jane.

"I still don't know how you did it," I replied.

"I realized very early on I had two choices: let fear overwhelm and consume me or find a way to deal with the brutal truth in front of me. I was literally confronted with this reality on a daily, if not hourly and minute-to-minute basis for two years, living face to face with every fear you can imagine.

He scratched his chin. "Funny thing about fear; it's a subconscious response, buried deep within our primal brains protecting us from our environment and the circumstances happening around us, and to us whatever it believes is dangerous. Back in the day when our ancestors were living in caves and being chased by saber-toothed tigers, the fear instinct was critical to their survival from being eaten alive! It's still there working when we feel threatened – you know, the fight, flight, or freeze mechanism. We need to consciously control our responses and not react and allow fear to control us. Fear feeds off repetition and we do it without thinking.

"Fear in many respects is like a fire: a small spark can turn into a raging inferno pretty quickly if it's not controlled. But like all things in life, it depends on which side of the fence you're sitting on. Call it the yin and yang of life if you like. Fire in and of itself isn't good or bad; it is good or bad depending on the circumstance. It can heat your home and provide the comforts of life – hot water, this delicious brisket, and a warm toasty fireplace. At the same time, the same fire can torch your house to the ground burning it into worthless ashes.

"Yeah, but that doesn't really help knowing my retirement account has been slashed in half and, as we speak, my financial world is sliding into the abyss," I retorted.

"Ah Chris, there you go again! You still have those saber tooth tiger fears buried in your mind. We create these stories in our minds. We paint these pictures of a fictitious future; we treat them like they are facts and believe with great certainty they will happen. Fear, you see, is a belief, a perception, and all beliefs and perceptions can be changed.

"Our perceptions, images, and stories are all manufactured in the imagination. Think of what a miraculous factory we have in our minds! Everything in your life, my life here in New York City, is a manifestation of someone's imagination. Someone somewhere thought up this building's blueprint, someone thought up the design for this sweater, even that frozen banana cream pie you brought over was formulated in the mind of someone. We can utilize the imagination machine in our minds for creative purposes; you just need to consciously create a vision of your future instead of allowing your fear to do it to you and for you."

Freddie had a tendency at times to veer off on a tangent and I was not afraid to let him know I wasn't following him. "What does that have to do with me losing my retirement?" I asked.

"I'm saying you are using your imagination in the wrong way. You are allowing it to create a future grounded in fear. You are manufacturing an image of your future which is completely fictional and believing it is going to happen. This is causing incredible unease in your life," he diagnosed. "It's bad now and that's where your focus is, but you don't know where the stock market will be in four, five, or six years? It's your perception of the event happening now that is creating the fear within you (Freddie's prescient words held true: as I'm writing this from the time we spoke in 2008 the Dow Jones Industrial average has tripled from 9,000 to 30,000!)

Freddie picked up his fork and speared the brisket off the plate. "Fear is like this brisket," Freddie said.

I looked at him strangely.

"I've heard of fear being compared to many things – but a brisket? That's the first time in the history of mankind I've heard of it," Jane remarked. We all laughed.

"No, think of it like this: the brisket, this beautiful piece of meat, tastes like heaven and smells even better. We love it, right? I mean it's one of my favorite dishes," Freddie exclaimed.

"Me, too. By the way it's delicious, Jane," I said smiling at her.

"Thank you, Chris," Jane replied kindly.

"The reality of this fantastic brisket is that at one point not too long ago it was a living cow, breathing, chewing away at its cud happily on a farm somewhere. Then it was dead. Now we're eating it. The stark reality is this brisket is dead cow flesh. That's the reality. Our perception of the brisket is highly different than the reality of being dead cow flesh. Fear in many ways is similar to that," Freddie explained thoughtfully.

I was starting to have second thoughts of that cute little baby cow that was running free in the fields with its cow friends and now I was eating it. I wondered what its name was?

Freddie changed the subject quickly and turned to me. "How did your two-day ashram go by the way – speaking of fear? Where did you wind up going?" he asked.

"My buddy has a cabin in the Catskills, so I spent a weekend up there," I told him.

"Did you bring the notebook?"

"Got it right here," I obliged as I pulled it out of my bag.

"Let's take a look." Freddie scanned my notes. "I see a lot of fear in your writing," he commented as he continued to browse through.

"Yeah I'm worried about a lot of things in my life, Freddie, not just the stock market. Fear of my future, losing the business, losing my fiancée, going into a totally unknown future," I continued to confess.

"And..." Freddie asked with a hint of impatience. "You know, Chris, everything you fear happened to me! I'll never forget that day. I was sitting at my kitchen table in Dallas with my lawyer sitting across from me as I signed my bankruptcy forms after having lost everything. Millions of dollars...gone, Chris! Just a few weeks before, I was sitting at the same table with the same lawyer signing my divorce papers. The feeling – in fact, it wasn't even a feeling – it was a flood, an overwhelming incomprehensible deluge of uncontrollable horror that was about to kill me.

"I had hard times in my life, like in Vietnam, but this fear and this reality were inhuman. My two daughters were gone along with my ex-wife, my business and real estate empire gone! I was totally alone and I was petrified. I didn't know what I was going to do," he said as he started to choke up.

I could tell Freddie had experienced not only fear but real tragedy in his life. Yet somehow I was sitting here with him listening to his life story, and I could tell he was a man content with the world.

"What did you do after that?" I asked, still processing how inconceivable one man's tragedies in life could be.

"After I lost the house, I lived in my car for a month trying to piece my life back together – and that's when I had an epiphany that changed my life forever. The sun beaming down through the window woke me up one morning after another night of sleeping in the backseat in my car. You know what? An overwhelming sense of freedom washed over me. I literally had $45 in my pocket and a suitcase in the trunk. And I was free! I was free from the fear of losing everything. It had already been lost! All my mental anguish seemed to just evaporate. To this day I still can't explain why I felt that way – I mean all my fears had become realities for me, Chris. But somehow all the emotional energy attached to them was gone. That's the strange phenomenon of fear: it's all an illusion."

I laughed under my breath after Freddie finished telling me his story, a little startled at my reaction to what he said. "Sorry for laughing, Freddie, it's not funny what happened to you. I just uh, well, I was laughing at myself really, I guess. All my fears are just eating me up in my own mind and imagination. But, in your case they actually happened to you!"

Freddie pulled out the now famous silver pen from his jacket pocket and grabbed a paper napkin and started drawing. He slid the napkin over to me as he explained the diagram he created. The first drawing was a series of three concentric circles. I looked at them bewildered. Across the top he wrote:

THE CIRCLE OF FEAR

"Here's what I want you to do, Chris. Write in the center of the circle any fear you are having. We talked about the fear of you losing your money and being homeless and destitute, right?" he established.

"Yeah, that's pretty scary," I admitted.

"So write down in the center circle:

FEAR OF BEING HOMELESS AND DESTITUTE

"Where do you think that fear comes from?" he asked.

"Probably from my childhood. We were always in trouble financially. I remember when I was just a kid, like ten or eleven, the banks calling the house saying they were going to foreclose on our home. I used to have nightmares as a child of being homeless. I've carried that fear with me since then," I disclosed.

"On top of the next circle write down:

WHAT PULLS ME INTO FEAR

"Think of the things that trigger your fear. For example, thinking of a future where you are destitute, obsessing over watching your IRA, obsessing about the market, worrying about future bills. Just brainstorm what your personal triggers are that get your mind racing about the fictitious future you are creating based on fear.

"At the top of the outer circle write:

WHAT I CAN DO TO CHANGE

"You can help others, start a new business, take a finance class on saving money and investing, learn a new skill to make money, get a part-time job, ya know, things that would alleviate the fear of being destitute. The idea is to get your mind thinking in a different direction regarding your fears," he explained.

"That's a lot of work, Freddie!" I protested.

"We're not done yet," he laughed. He pointed to the next picture he'd drawn on the napkin.

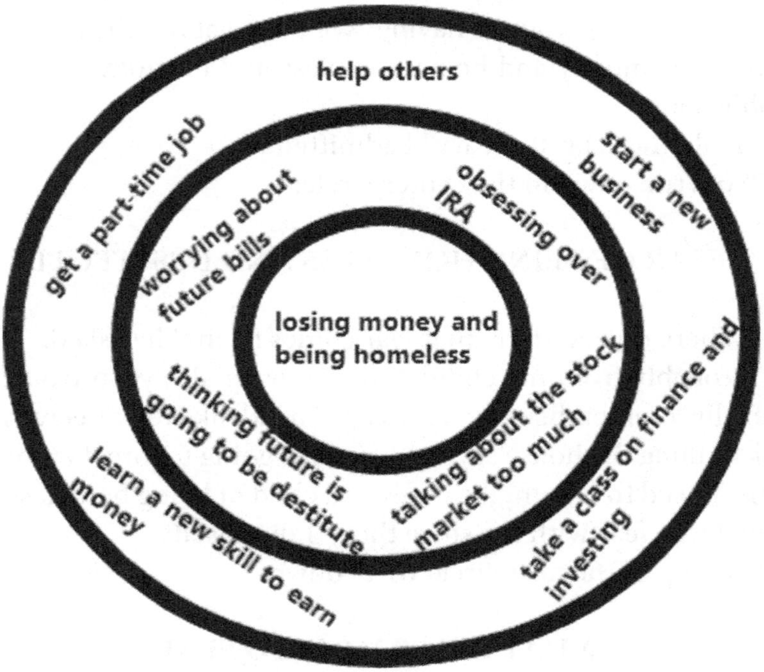

The top of the diagram read:

THE CLINT EASTWOOD TEST

"OK, this is called the Clint Eastwood Test. He was in a great movie called *The Good the Bad and the Ugly*. Ever seen it?" he asked.

"No," I exclaimed. "When was it made?"

"I dunno; let me check. He pulls out his phone and looks it up. 1966, a wonderful year!"

"I was negative three years old, Freddie," I said.

"OK. Well, the point is whenever you have any fear around a decision, you can run it through the Clint Eastwood Test. It's a simple way to look at any choice you have to make in three different ways, that's all. Do it for all your stocks or any decision where there is uncertainty and you feel frozen or fearful. For example, think about your fear of losing your IRA. What's one of the stocks you own?" he asked.

"IBM. Why?" I asked.

"Let's take a look at it," as he pointed to three columns he created:

THE GOOD THE BAD THE UGLY

"You're afraid of the stock losing value, right?" he said.

"Yeah."

"What would be a good or great scenario to happen to the stock?" he asked.

"Good or great case scenario: it comes back and goes higher from what I bought it at," I told him.

"What is the likelihood of that happening?"

"Not sure really," I said.

"Think about each scenario and then simply assign a probability to it based on what you think might be a reasonable outcome.

It helps to take some of the emotion out of the decisions," Freddie reasoned.

"I don't know, maybe 70 percent," I responded.

"OK, that's sounds reasonable. Write that down. What would be a bad scenario?" he asked.

"Bad...it stays down and I lose some money and it never gets back to what I bought it for. I'd give that, say, 20 percent."

"And, finally, what would be the ugliest, or worst-case scenario," he asked.

"Ugly. The company goes out of business and I lose all my money. Not likely, say,

10 percent," I calculated.

Freddie busily scribbled on the napkin as I rattled off my probabilities and

scenarios.

THE GOOD	THE BAD	THE UGLY
The stock does comes back and goes higher from where you bought 70%	It stays down and you lose some money. It never gets back to what you bought 20%	The company goes out of business – lose all money 10%

"Apply the probabilities, make your decision and you can stop worrying about it. Let it go, knowing you've analyzed different scenarios and are going with the best odds," Freddie concluded.

I was getting used to Freddie's homework assignments and they were beginning to make sense. I understood he had a certain view of the world and I could maybe gain a different perspective on my life and the events that were happening to me.

"Oh, another thing, Chris, remember...yahoo," Freddie advised as we were wrapping up the dinner.

"Yahoo? The chocolate milk?" I said unsure of where we were going.

"No, the acronym YAHOO – You Always Have Optimistic Options," he said, wrapping up with a smile.

Yahoo, Circle of Fear, Clint Eastwood Test, and I still haven't eaten brisket since that day at Freddie's apartment.

Chapter Sixteen

THE MOST PRECIOUS COMMODITY

You live as if you were destined to live forever; no thought of your frailty ever enters your head; of how much time has already gone by, you take no heed. You squander time as if you drew from a full and abundant supply, though all the while that day which you bestow on some person or thing is perhaps your last.

~ *Seneca*

Friday night arrived and I met up with Freddie at a local greasy spoon diner in Battery Park down the street from my apartment. They had the best Denver omelets in the city. We got a booth by the window away from the main dining room. I knew we were going to be having some heavy conversations tonight and I didn't want to have to talk over the noise.

"Pretty cool diner," said Freddie, "I haven't been to Battery Park in a few years."

"I'll give you a little history about Battery Park," I told him. "It used to be controlled by the Lenape Indians until the Dutch took it over in the 17th century. The Lenape Indians were all over

Delaware, Pennsylvania, New Jersey and parts of New York. My ancestors were Quakers who left England in the 1600s due to religious persecution and came to America. They landed in Delaware and lived in caves to survive the brutal winter. The Lenape Indians brought them food and clothing and kept them alive."

"So you wouldn't be here if it wasn't for the Lenape Indians is what you are saying?" Freddie said.

"I would say so. Because of their kindness to my ancestors, I'm here talking to you," I said.

"See what happens when you plant those seeds of kindness, Chris? You might not see the rewards right away, but they will eventually show up. The Lenape who helped your family couldn't have foreseen what their actions would have done to future generations, but here you are today with me having an awesome Denver omelet because of those small acts of kindness 400 years ago by complete strangers," Freddie mused. "I think all those bankers on Wall Street would say that's a pretty good return on investment. They always talk about the time value of money. I 'm talking about the time value of kindness," he said with a sagacious look.

"You're right, Freddie. I wouldn't be here without the help of complete strangers. They had no ulterior motives; just being kind to others because we are here together on the planet."

"Now you're getting it, kid. Strangers helping strangers without expecting anything in return – that's what's going to save humanity," he said with a smile.

Freddie broke out an inhaler and took a giant hit.

"I didn't know you used one of those," I said.

"Yeah, I was a smoker for thirty years. Been abstinent for the past four years, but sometimes my emphysema flares up," he said. "I probably wouldn't have quit if it wasn't for my wife. She'd been trying to get me to stop for years; I just couldn't kick it. The patch, hypnosis…nothing worked. Then one day she told me she had a surprise for me. She brought me down to the morgue and had one of the doctors show me a patient who had died of lung cancer from smoking. The cadaver was opened up on the table and I could see the diseased lungs right there in front of me. The doctor told me that was going to be me in a few years if I didn't stop smoking.

I almost threw up right there. I was so disgusted with myself, Chris. I knew what he was saying was true. I walked out of the morgue and haven't picked up a cigarette since. It's been almost four years, but I'm still dealing with the ramifications of thirty years of abusing my lungs. Battling early-stage emphysema, but the doctors think my lungs are starting to heal. My breathing is definitely getting better; but sometimes it gets bad and the inhaler helps."

"Glad to hear it. That's quite a way to make you quit. I'll have to give Jane kudos next time I see her," I said.

"Every time I breathe into this thing, it reminds me my time is running out. It makes me think of a riddle:

I never was, am always to be,
No one ever saw me, nor ever will,
And yet I am the confidence of all
To live and breathe on this terrestrial ball.

"You know what it is?" he asked.

"No idea," I said pondering.

"Tomorrow. Tomorrow is the answer."

"What does that have to do with me?" I asked.

"Just bringing it up. Most people get caught up in the disease of 'tomorrow.' They are living like they have an infinite number of tomorrows, but the truth is they don't. They waste today, the most precious gift they have. They're going to lose the weight tomorrow, they're going to quit smoking tomorrow, they're going to apologize tomorrow, they're going to change jobs tomorrow, they're going to start the business tomorrow. Whatever the 'it' is, they are going to do it tomorrow. I'm just saying you're not guaranteed tomorrow at all.

"Think about all those people in the World Trade Center back on 9/11; no one would have thought that could have happened. One minute they were making big plans for their future, the next minute the towers were falling. Life can change in a split second. You don't know how much time you have left; that's why it is so important to be grateful for today and utilize your time wisely... TODAY. You can always make more money, but you can only lose time. As Benjamin Franklin said, 'Lost time is never found.'

He turned to me, "Think about this: how old are you, Chris?"

"Thirty-seven. Why?"

"OK, for argument's sake let's say you're going to live another thirty-three years – you'll be about seventy, right?"

"Well, let's hope it's longer," I laughingly replied.

Freddie pulled out his phone and started typing. "So thirty-three years, in twenty-four hours you spend eight hours sleeping. One-third of your life. So that puts you at roughly eleven years sleeping so you are basically unconscious for the next third of your life, so you have twenty-two years of 'living' left. The average American spends thirty-five hours a week watching TV, and depending on your age, about two hours a day on social media. Let's just say it's forty hours a week on entertainment. That's about seven and a half years – let's just round up and say eight years of entertaining yourself. So now you have about fourteen years of time left. Let's say you're working eight hours a day plus traveling roughly two hours a day – that's ten hours. That's around nine and a half years – ten to make it easier. Now you have about four years left. Eating let's say takes an hour a day. That's about one and a half years. How much time socializing? Going to friends' houses, talking on the phone, playing golf – whatever. Let's say two hours a week – that's about a half a year, putting you around two years. When you have kids, forget it; now you have no time left," Freddie calculated.

"It's a scary concept when you think about it," I admitted.

"On top of all that, we ain't guaranteed tomorrow. So many of us take time for granted. Like I had a sense of urgency to quit smoking, you need to develop a sense of urgency about losing and wasting time. Most people don't realize how little time they have left until something catastrophic happens: they get diagnosed with a terminal disease or have a severe accident, or they get shot in a war. Whatever it is, don't wait for that to happen! Take control of your time and life now! People spend more time planning their vacations than planning their lives.

He looked serious. "What is the main thing you want to accomplish with your time here on earth? Gotta get clear on what you want and why you want it. You're staying stuck in this relationship and in this business, hoping it's going to turn around. What if it doesn't? What if it gets worse? You can turn it around now and pursue the life you really want. The time to get it done is now, and make it happen.

"You know, when I was in real estate there was an adage called 'highest and best use.' I would always be asking myself 'What is the highest and best use' of this particular parcel or building? In the same vein, you need to be constantly asking yourself, 'What is the highest and best use of my time in this current moment?' All you really have is the right here, right now moment in front of you. Invest in it wisely," he ended.

"Now, are you ready for some homework?" And Freddie brought out the silver pen and started writing on the napkin lying in front of him.

"This might seem like a strange exercise, but I think it will help transform your perspective on time. Do you know where Calvary Cemetery is?"

"No, why?" I remarked surprised.

"Look it up; it's the largest cemetery in New York and maybe the United States. I want you to go there for an afternoon, walk around and take it in for what it is."

"You want me to spend a whole afternoon wandering around a cemetery? Isn't that a waste of time?"

"In this case – no. It's your homework assignment. I want you to feel what is there, to understand what it means to be buried and dead. It's a long time and it's forever! It will help you comprehend the absolute brevity of your existence here on earth and help you see time as a gift from God or the Universe or whatever you choose to believe. Appreciate it, invest in it, cherish it, guard it, because once it's gone, it's gone forever.

"And, while you're there, take a look at some of the epitaphs and start thinking about what you want to have written on your tombstone."

"Jeez, Freddie, now you are starting to freak me out a little," I replied.

"Remember how the vision of the diseased lungs scared me sober from cigarettes?" "How could I forget!"

"Well this exercise is designed to do the same. To scare you, or awaken you, to the reality that time is flying by, and that you really don't have much time left. Once you become aware viscerally of the reality of time, you can live backwards from death."

"What do you mean?"

"In other words, when you internalize the reality of your own mortality, life takes on a whole new meaning. When you start living backwards from the end, every moment takes on a new meaning with an inherent value you might have taken for granted otherwise."

"Calvary Cemetery? Epitaphs? Tombstones?"

"Now you're getting it! Besides, like I always say: what's the worst that could happen?"

Chapter Seventeen

GRATITUDE IN ATTITUDE

> Reflect upon your present blessings, of which every man has plenty; not on your past misfortunes, of which all men have some.
>
> ~ *Charles Dickens*

All of my Fridays with Freddie were showing up in my thoughts and perceptions. I was seeing the reality of my life for what it was, not how I wished it to be. I knew I had a dream that I wasn't living out, and time wasn't on my side. If I was going to do something with my life, I had to take ownership of it and make the change.

I sent Freddie an email during the week informing him I was moving to California. This Friday would be our last meeting together and I thanked him for all he had done for me.

Friday morning Freddie called letting me know he had a memorable going away present for me and told me to bring a special friend. I invited Marie to join me for my last Friday with Freddie, and we met up with him and Jane at Chelsea Piers. Freddie had bought tickets for a dinner riverboat cruise around Manhattan. As usual, Freddie was dressed impeccably, wearing some famous designer I probably couldn't pronounce anyway even if I knew who it was. Jane looked equally magnificent wearing an elegant midnight blue dress that glittered and sparkled in the moonlight. Her immaculate snow-white hair rivaled Freddie's. They were made for this night.

It was a perfect evening for a cruise around the city. Not a cloud in the sky. A live band played soft jazz in the background as we headed up the Hudson River. The whiff of the saltwater from the ocean mixed with the aroma of the steaks sizzling from the kitchen wafted to our table as I sipped my seltzer with a twist of lime. The majesty of the Manhattan skyline was the perfect backdrop for the perfect evening. A magical moment indeed! There was nowhere else I would rather have been at that particular moment.

We hadn't been on the river more than ten minutes before Freddie was up and dancing. Apparently no matter where he was at any time with his wife, if he heard *The Girl from Ipanema* he got up and danced. She told me he even did it one time while they were riding the subway! Freddie was never going to miss an opportunity to have a good time. As soon as the song started, he broke away in mid-sentence and dragged Jane onto the dance floor.

They came back to the table holding hands, all smiles. I looked over at Freddie and

saw the same childlike wonder I'd seen in him before as he stared out the window at the glowing lights of the city. I could tell he was reflecting on something profound.

"This is the perfect evening, Freddie, thank you," I said. Marie thanked him as well.

He turned to me with a giant grin on his face, "I dunno, Chris, the last time I was on a river in a boat..." We both laughed knowingly. Jane leaned over to Marie and whispered, "They have an inside joke between the two of them. Don't worry, I don't get it either."

Freddie pulled me aside away from the table and handed me an envelope. "Here's a little going away present for ya, Chris," he said.

I slowly peeled open the envelope and inside was a bank check made out to me for $5,000.

"What's this?" I asked in disbelief.

"I stopped by Amir's brother's house and Amir and I had a conversation about the software project."

"You actually went to his house?" I asked incredulously.

"Hey, we gotta get an answer one way or another with this software project. Like I always say, nothing ventured, nothing gained, right?"

"I guess so. What made him give you this $5,000?" I asked again with the same disbelief.

"Well, we sat down and had a conversation. Needless to say, he was a little shocked to see me, but I let him know I'd spoken with his wife, or soon to be ex-wife, and she told me where to find him. I just let him know you and Steve wanted to find out about the project and the money and everything else. Not to get into the weeds, but he basically told me he'd run out of money and had used some of the funds from the project to pay off his lawyer for the divorce. I reasoned with him, and he met me halfway on getting your investment back. So there's half your money. I already gave Steve his five grand. I would write off the other $5000 to a 'learning experience.' A little costly, but a lesson you won't be forgetting anytime in the near future."

I was speechless. "I don't know what to say…thanks, Freddie."

"Anything for my friends," he replied with his hallmark smile. Freddie picked up his glass and made a toast. "Here's to new beginnings, here's to new friendships, here's to the beauty of this moment tonight! All the best luck with your new life in California, Chris! We wanted to leave you with a good memory and give you a going away present before you left for California."

We all clinked glasses.

"Look at all this," he said as he pointed to the skyline, "The creation of the human mind. Amazing! We created this. Humans, not dogs or cats or dolphins. We did it. We're lucky to experience it. Imagine we were born 1,000 years ago? We wouldn't have this moment – we'd be working on some farm somewhere probably and living in a grass hut or something. Gotta have gratitude if for nothing else but being born in this time and place in eternity in this moment," Freddie proclaimed.

"Or we're living in the jungles of Vietnam," I said with a wry smile as I winked at Freddie.

"Or we could be dead," Marie blurted out awkwardly and then cupped her mouth. I could tell she probably felt it was a little heavy for such a setting at such a time. She didn't know Freddie like I did.

"Speaking of death, Chris, how was your trip to the graveyard? Did you find the richest man in the cemetery?" Freddie asked.

I was a little embarrassed to be talking about my little excursion through the cemetery in front of Marie and Jane.

Marie looked at me with her head tilted to the side as if to ask whether she'd heard him correctly? "You went to a graveyard? For what reason, if you don't mind my asking? The richest man? You're starting to freak me out now, Chris, walking around graveyards looking for the richest man," she teased.

"It was a project Freddie gave me. I..."

Freddie interrupted me to explain the situation to Marie. "I told him to go to the graveyard and find the richest man there. I was trying to make the point that he shouldn't worry and wear himself out. We all end up in the same place, so enjoy your life while you have it. People don't like talking about death, but it is the only real truth we have in life. It's guaranteed to happen to everyone and everything. I'm not being morbid; in fact, quite the opposite. It gives you a greater sense of appreciation for your time now, knowing it won't be forever. We need to live with gratitude... gratitude in attitude. It's a practice we can develop.

He leaned over to Marie, "We were having a long conversation about changing his life and I was trying to make a point for him to realize how little time he had left. Hence the graveyard exercise."

"Okaaaaay, I get it – the graveyard exercise. I'm sure it's a long story. Chris can explain later," Marie replied.

"What did you learn, or should I say, experience, Chris?" Freddie asked me.

"Well I uh, first of all didn't find the richest man obviously. I can't believe how many people are there by the way. It seemed to go on for eternity. So many people, some old, far too many too young lying in their graves. I have been deceiving myself about how much time I have left on the planet. The point is if I'm going to be happy, or at least try to be, I need to pursue my dream," I admitted.

"Did you write your epitaph?" Freddie asked.

"Well I got one, but it isn't original. I saw it on a tombstone and wrote it down. I think it's a good way to live," I told him. I googled it and found that it was written by William Penn back in the 1700s but I think it's fitting for my life. If I could live my life in this way, I think I would have lived a purposeful meaningful life in spite of whatever happens. It goes like this:

> 'I expect to pass through this world but once. Any good, therefore, that I can do or any kindness I can show to any fellow creature, let me do it now. Let me not defer or neglect it, for I shall not pass this way again.'

"That would be a nice legacy if you could live like that, Chris, but you have a lot of work to do," Marie said to me as she softly punched me on the shoulder. The whole table laughed.

The band started playing Frank Sinatra's *Summer Wind*. Freddie jumped up, took Jane by the hand and made his way to the dance floor again. Apparently, *Girl from Ipanema* wasn't the only song Freddie needed an excuse to dance to.

"Come on, Chris, get up and dance – you only live once!" Freddie shouted as he tripped toward the dance floor. Up until that moment, I don't think I had danced since I took up break dancing at thirteen. I looked over at Marie. "What do you think... wanna dance?"

"Sure," she smiled. We got up and joined Freddie and Jane on the dance floor. I felt like a teenager again. Free! No worries in the world! Exhilarating! Not just the experience; it was my ability to allow myself to see it, to feel it, to be present and sculpt a magical moment in time. What else is there in life? Isn't time just a series of events one preceding the other? Why not try to make them all magical? Or at least be grateful for each one we have. After all, they're the only ones we will ever have.

We made our way back to our table just in time to see our meals being placed on the table. We sat down and as usual paused silently before eating.

"What a perfect night to be alive, right guys!" Freddie declared. "I'm grateful we are able to be here and share it together." He motioned to me, "Chris, what are you grateful for tonight?"

"I can dance. I haven't done that since I was a kid. I forgot how fun it was."

"You're pretty good, I might add, but Freddie, I don't know, needs a little work," Jane joked. Everyone at the table laughed.

"Marie, how about you?" Freddie asked.

"Glad I'm able to be here with you guys tonight and experience this moment with friends...It's amazing!" she replied clasping her hands together.

"Jane, how about you?" Freddie asked.

"If you couldn't see the city, see this incredible skyline, it would have no value. If you couldn't smell the steaks and you couldn't taste them, they wouldn't have any value. And, of course, being with the love of my life on this beautiful night," she exclaimed as she pinched Freddie's cheek.

"I was just about to say that, honey; that was my next line!" Freddie exclaimed. We all laughed. "You probably all feel better now."

"What about you, Freddie? What are you grateful for most in your life," Marie quizzed him.

"Check this out," Freddie said excitedly as he pulled out his wallet, reached in and pried open a crumpled folded piece of paper that looked like it was a hundred years old. "I've been carrying this around with me since I was in Vietnam. Marie, did you know you can manufacture happiness?" Freddie asked.

"No, I didn't know that," she answered, somewhat off guard.

"I wrote it down over forty years ago and still carry it with me today. I wrote ten things I was grateful for, no matter how dark my life got, what was beautiful in my life in spite of whatever was going on around me, no matter how hopeless it seemed. I would read and recite my list out loud several times every day, reminding myself what I was grateful for. I still do it to this day."

He opened up the paper and laid it out on the table so we could see what he wrote.

At the top it read:

WHAT I'M GRATEFUL FOR

1. I'm alive.
2. I can see.
3. I can think.
4. My brother and friends care about me.
5. I can walk.
6. I live in America.
7. I have water and food.
8. Sunsets and sunrises.
9. Got a full head of hair.
10. I can read.

"I know it sounds simple, but you wouldn't believe how helpful it is to have a list of things you are grateful for, especially when you are in the throes of darkness.

"When I'm feeling down, need an attitude adjustment or I don't have the list with me, I just cycle through my finger exercise. Each finger represents something I'm grateful for, like a mantra to alter my thoughts. I do this." Freddie started touching his fingers together on his right hand first touching his thumb to his pinky, then his thumb to his ring finger, his thumb to his middle finger and then his thumb to his index finger twice, then doing the same on his left hand. Each time he did that he would recite what he was grateful for: "One – I'm alive, two – I can see, three – I can think, continuing with his list up to ten."

Freddie continued. "You see we are programmed from a young age to think negatively. So, if you aren't practicing gratitude, worry, fear and doubt will infect and infiltrate your attitudes and thoughts and, ultimately, your actions. We have to stage a conscious fight against them to reprogram our minds. Gratitude is a practice: it's tangible; it's something that we can change, develop and cultivate."

He looked around. "There are people who could be on this cruise with us right now who couldn't or wouldn't see the beauty of it. They'll complain about the view, or the music, the food or whatever. Gratitude in attitude is everything people!" Freddie declared.

"It's all a state of mind, right Freddie?" I chipped in.

"That's the ticket. You can choose to see the goodness in life in any and all situations; it just takes a little practice that's all," he smiled.

As Freddie was talking, the boat pulled into the dock back at Chelsea Piers.

"I'll leave you with this," he smiled at me as he reached into his jacket one last time and pulled out his silver pen. He turned over his paper and started scribbling on the back. He handed me his list of the ten things he was grateful for he had written down while in Vietnam, "Here Chris, I want you to have this," he said, sliding the paper across the table to me.

It read:

> Cultivate the habit of being grateful for every good thing that comes to you, and give thanks continuously. And, because all

things have contributed to your advancement, you should include all things in your gratitude.

Ralph Waldo Emerson

1.
2.
3.
4.
5.
6.
7.
8.
9.
10.

He looked at me intently with this parting word: "When things get rough in California – and they will – that's a guarantee. It's part of the process. Remember Gratitude in Attitude no matter what is going on in your life: that's the key. Make a list of ten things that you're grateful for. Really think about it. Personalize it. Carry it with you like I did. Practice the finger gratitude exercises many times a day and you will see your thoughts start to shift. It works, trust me."

I sat speechless staring at the paper. Once again, Freddie gave me a gift I knew had incredible sentimental value to him. It took all I had within me to hold back how I was feeling at that moment. Freddie had come into my life a total stranger, and here we were parting ways as best friends. He helped me find the courage to make the changes to move forward in my life in spite of all the obstacles and fears that stood in the way. Tonight would be a night etched in my memory forever as I wrote the next chapter of my life in the Golden State.

Chapter Eighteen

GO CONFIDENTLY IN THE DIRECTION OF YOUR DREAMS

> I learned that courage was not the absence of fear, but the triumph over it. The brave man is not he who does not feel afraid but he who conquers that fear.
>
> ~ *Nelson Mandela*

I reached out to a friend of mine in California and told him of my plans to move out and he more than agreed to help me get situated once I got out there. I packed whatever I could into a U-Haul and sold or threw out whatever else I had accumulated over the course of my life. It's amazing how much junk we collect. It seems to have a life of its own like it gives birth to other junk and keeps piling up.

I took a deep breath and called my ex-fiancée in Switzerland and gave her two weeks' notice. She was startled – to say the least. She definitely didn't think I would walk away from the company we had built together over the last ten years. But my sanity was on the line and I knew if I stayed any longer it would only get worse. Much worse. I had to walk away to save myself.

We had a business contract which spelled out the terms of what and how we would divide the company in the event either one of us decided we wanted out. I figured we would just work it out long distance. Freddie had helped to show me a better way for my life and I was going to follow it, no matter the consequences.

I had started the process of letting go, and the first part of that equation was leaving New York City! Once I got to California, I figured my head would clear up a little bit, knowing I was out of the swamp and one step closer to the vision of my new future. I would have to let the chips fall where they may and have faith and hope in the courage "to go confidently in the direction of my dreams."

PART II

TWELVE YEARS LATER

Chapter Nineteen

A TWIST OF FORTUNE

> Go confidently in the direction of your dreams! Live the life you've imagined.
>
> ~ *Henry David Thoreau*

I followed my vision of becoming a writer and moved to Hollywood to make it happen. Freddie and I stayed in touch for a few years after I left New York, but as things often do in the course of life, we drifted apart as time passed save for the seasonal Christmas emails and birthday texts.

All that was about to change.

It was January 2020 and all my hard work seemed to be paying off. I had been in Hollywood grinding away at my dream for twelve years, writing in Starbucks, writing at the beach, writing everywhere and anywhere I could, submitting treatments for my screenplays, taking writing classes, hiring a writing coach, begging everyone I knew who knew someone who might know someone who was "in the business" to read my scripts.

In a way I sort of missed the directness of New Yorkers. People in Hollywood were so passive- aggressive. Anytime anyone read my scripts, the feedback was almost always the same: "I really like your stuff; you have a lot of talent. I especially like what you did with ____ fill in the blanks – dialogue, character development, whatever – but it needs a little work." It was as if they passed around cards in Hollywood with what to tell people to politely reject their screenplays. Everyone had the same answer. In New York they would have told me the raw truth about how they felt and moved on to the next topic of conversation, or they would have just thrown me out of their office.

I wrote five movies and a TV pilot, spent virtually all my savings from the sale of my shares of the company I owned with my ex-fiancée, and worked endless odd jobs, as most do in Hollywood: telemarketing selling everything from toner to home improvement to solar panels. I was making just enough to pay my bills, so I could spend the rest of my time writing. I finally found an agent and got "the call" from her that a couple of producers had shown interest in one of my scripts and wanted to talk further.

My dream was unfolding, albeit a little longer than I had desired – but that was OK. I had been seriously dating a woman for the last five years and I found myself having a second conversation about possibly getting married. Life was good, definitely better than the last time I spoke with Freddie. But I had forgotten the golden rule for life that Seneca taught 2000 years ago:

> Cling tooth and nail to the following rule: Not to give in to adversity, never to trust prosperity, and always take full note of fortune's habit of behaving just as she pleases, treating her as if she were actually going to do everything it is in her power to do.

How could I when everything was flying in my direction? The momentum seemed unstoppable. Then it all ceased – at the drop of a dime. It was over. The phone stopped ringing, my agent stopped taking my calls, I lost my job. Everything ended. As quickly as the good news hit, the really bad news hit: Covid-19 crashed on the country like a tsunami.

I couldn't believe what was happening. No one in our lifetime had ever seen or imagined something like that. Ford stopped making cars! Airplanes stopped flying! It was surreal. Hollywood stopped production of everything! Life in America and around the world came to a screeching halt – literally!

What was I to do? I had just turned fifty and it was all gone. When the lockdown hit, I felt strangely disconnected from humanity. I frantically called to reconnect and touch base with friends both close and distant, family members, childhood buddies, old college roommates. And, of course, there was Freddie.

In the midst of the Covid insanity, I had to move out of where I was living with my girlfriend. She lost her job and just couldn't handle the stress of Covid; she nearly had a nervous breakdown. My friend had a small sailboat in Marina Del Rey he could rent to me until I found another place to live, so I threw my stuff in storage, packed my bags, and moved my life into my new home. I had no running water, but it was cheap and gave me some time to recoup and figure out what I was going to do next with my life.

I was lost, almost literally at sea, and I needed my North Star. Time to talk to Freddie!

Chapter Twenty

ADJUSTING ONE'S SAILS

> Just keep in mind: the more we value things outside our control, the less control we have.
>
> ~ *Epictetus*

I called Freddie. Of course it was Friday. I wasn't superstitious, but I figured it couldn't hurt. I was worried about him; I knew he was getting up in age and was a vulnerable candidate for COVID-19, so it was so good to hear his voice again. We picked up like it was just another Friday in a diner in New York City.

"Hey Chris, how ya been?" Freddie greeted me with his typical excitement.

"Well…it's a long story, Freddie," I said.

"Hey, I got time," he replied.

"More importantly, how are you doing?" I asked.

"Well I just turned seventy-three and I'm feeling great. I can't believe it. Seems like we were having dinner at my apartment in the city just yesterday. So crazy! I have a brand-new granddaughter who is five months old and my grandson just turned seven. They're adorable. It looks like I picked up a second career as a home health attendant, not officially, but I'm doing the work. My brother Lloyd just moved in with me. He's got terminal brain cancer, so I've been taking care of him as well, helping him get around to doctors and with his medicine. My health is good save for a few nicks and tweaks here and there, but thank God I feel great. Life keeps rolling on and I'm rolling with it," he said with a laugh.

Classic Freddie, practicing what he preached! He was there to help anyone who needed him without expecting anything in return. I was so glad to hear from him and that he was still doing well.

"Are you still in California? Staying out of the way of this crazy virus?" he asked.

"I'm living on a small 1976 sailboat in Marina del Rey. I have no running water, collecting unemployment. I'm basically homeless. It's all gone, Freddie. The virus took everything," I told him in a faltering voice.

"Sounds like you are going through another storm," he said.

"Yeah, a couple of 'em. Seems like every area in my life is getting hammered. It's horrible. I've lost everything I've worked for in the last twelve years. I got so close, Freddie, so close. I had an agent, was getting traction on a script, and I could see my dream unfolding in front of me when it all happened."

"What are you going to do?"

"I don't know, Freddie; I'm devastated. It's all up in smoke. This Covid thing hit fast and hard and caught me off guard," I said.

"Heck, it caught the whole world off guard. You built your life and got wiped out. It happens; it's part of life. Doesn't happen to everyone but it happens in life. As you know, it happened to me twice!

"The question is: are you going to stay stuck in the past, drowning in your emotions of regret and whatever else you are feeling, and ruminating on what you lost? Are you going about complaining? Are you going to worry about your future based on negative images, fearful and doubtful expectations, and worst-case scenarios? Are you going to let what is going on around you define you, crush you, cripple you and sink your ship? You have a choice how you are going to respond to current events.

"This isn't the first storm you've faced in life and won't be the last. Gotta learn to adjust your sails to the shifting winds, my friend," Freddie said in that all too familiar tone.

"It's not just the winds that are shifting. I'm getting hit with tidal waves, sharks are circling my boat, and lightning just struck the mast," I blurted out. "That's what's going on in my life."

"The winds of change will blow in the direction they choose. Your job now is to adjust your sails to the changing weather. Adjust your sails to the changing tides and waves of adversity. Adapt to the new reality, new information, new challenges and adopt new initiatives. If there were no winds of adversity in your life, your sailboat would stay stuck in the harbor, rotting and rusting away. You wouldn't be able to see the majesty of the open seas. The winds give lift to your boat, and in the same way, adversity gives lift to you – if you allow it to. You see where I'm going with this?" he asked.

As usual Freddie was dropping some heavy wisdom on me, but I wasn't in the
mood. "Freddie that's a beautiful metaphor but I'm in a bad way. It's all over," I moaned.

"Or it's all getting started, depending on how you look at it," he responded.

Knowing Freddie the way I did, I could feel him smiling through the phone.

"I know how you feel - believe me I understand, I've been in way worse situations
than you are in now, and I'm telling you how I got through them. Often, we can't see how our situation will actually be a blessing in disguise in the future.

"The two nightmare scenarios in my life, surviving the hell out of the Vietnam War and going bankrupt and losing everything – my family, my business, my fortune – have all now become blessings in my life. I couldn't have seen it then, but now I spend a lot of my time helping other veterans with PTSD work through their trauma from various wars, not just Vietnam. Now, like I told you before, I'm my ex-wife's best friend and I'm able to be there for her. So you see, in many ways, it's like the story about the horse and the farmer I told you about twelve years ago. You remember it?"

"How could I forget," I told him sheepishly. I knew he wasn't going to let me wallow again, drowning in fear, worry, and self-pity. "What do I do? I don't even know where to start?" I asked.

"Now, first things first; where are your feet at?" he asked.

"I'm on a boat in the Marina del Rey."

"That doesn't sound too bad, living in the marina on a boat, not having to work for a

while," he chuckled. "Life could be worse, right?"

"I guess so," I replied.

"Can you still think, work, study? Do you have access to the internet?"

"Of course," I told him.

"So there are positive things going on. You're just not acknowledging them or

seeing them for what they are. You need to frame the situation differently and not process it through a negative emotional lens that gets distorted by what is happening in front of you. It's going to cloud your judgment. I'm not saying your feelings aren't real and aren't powerful – they are. You just need to navigate them wisely.

"Remember, your will is stronger than your emotions. You are *not* your feelings. You have been reacting to situations emotionally. The objective is to learn to detach and observe the emotion from a distance, not to *be* it. Tell yourself you are in a state, be it mental, emotional, physical, financial, whatever it is. You are not fear or depression any more than you are water when you are in the ocean. You are in a wet state when you are in the water. As in all things, you will cycle in and out of states. You will get out of the water and dry off; then you will be in a dry state. The idea is not to get stuck and to find ways to pull yourself out of negative states.

"Always getting the true perspective, right, Freddie," I reminded him.

"It's all you've got. Can't control the virus. Can't control the economy. When I was struggling in Vietnam and fear and worry were closing in and it seemed totally unbearable, I would reprogram my mind and tell myself this over and over: 'I am in Vietnam, I feel uncomfortable, I'm hungry, cold and wet, it's dangerous. But this will end one day, and I am going to do whatever it takes to survive and build an amazing life when I get out.'

"Get a pen, Chris, and write this down. I wish I had the napkin for this," he joked. We both laughed.

"Write down: 'I am ___. I feel ___ the situation is ___. I'm going to do ___ to get to

__. ' Frame your situation in writing so you have it in front of you. When you write it out and verbalize what you are feeling and what is going on around you, it helps to reposition the situation in your mind, so your brain isn't swamped by the negativity of your emotions.

"Create your mantra now on how you're going to reframe your current position. For example: you are on the boat, you feel upset and fear losing all you've worked for and for your future. The situation is unstable. However, you are now going to redefine and recreate your new life in spite of your circumstances to get to where you want to be...a successful writer, for example. When your mind starts drifting into negative emotions –

and we know it will – recite your new mantra over and over to steer your mind back into a stronger, more positive state.

"Remember how we talked about living with one hand reaching down to help someone, and one hand reaching up to ask for help and to keep looking up to a higher, brighter, better future? We can't do it without the help of others and without helping others. Ask your way to success.

"I know it's tough to do anything now; you probably can't get to a homeless shelter to teach computers like you were doing in

New York. But why don't you pick your favorite charity and write them a check?" he suggested.

"A check?" I asked, somewhat confused.

"Whatever you feel comfortable with. Remember, kindness is God's currency and the return on investment is guaranteed. Put it out and it comes back multiplied. Remember the Lenape, how they helped your ancestors four hundred years ago? You are benefiting from their acts of kindness now. Return the favor. It comes back to us often at times when we don't expect it to.

"At least coming from that state of mind you will have a much better chance of recreating your life going forward. Again, you're telling yourself subconsciously that you care about others and you're getting outside your own feelings of fear of not having enough control over your life."

"Money's kind of tight right now," I exclaimed trying to sneak out of another one of Freddie's homework assignments.

"That's the point. You don't want the fear of having no money to control you. Now's your chance to help someone in their own cave during the pandemic, the way the Lenape helped your ancestors when they lived in a cave. Ain't gonna kill ya Chris. Besides, what's the worst that could happen? Call me next Friday and let me know how things are coming along."

Chapter Twenty-One

THE POWER OF TEN

Decide what you want, decide what you are willing to exchange for it. Establish your priorities and go to work.

~ *H.L Hunt*

I was swimming in my head and my mind was scrambled. No job, living on a small boat with no running water and nowhere to go, I could feel the old ghosts of depression knocking on the door of my soul. The enormity of the collapse and devastation was starting to gnaw at me. I was losing hope about what was unfolding around me.

Freddie must have had a sixth sense about what I was going through because he called me at an ungodly hour Friday morning and woke me up.

"How ya doin, kid?" he asked.

"Pretty good. Hanging in there," I said blandly. I tried to hide my fear and brewing paranoia.

He saw right through it. "Sounds like something's bothering you. What's going on?" he asked.

I knew from past experiences that being honest with Freddie was the best way to work through my feelings and my life.

"I'm starting to freak out about what's going on. I'm not handling this too well. It's just right now it seems like everything is collapsing around me."

"Your dream of building a screenwriting career and having a successful life as a writer has been derailed. Welcome to the human race! Lots of people around the world are now in a new reality – and it's not the one they wanted or planned," he said. "We're in unique times – basically we're at war."

"It is war, or certainly seems like it," I said. "If you think about it, Covid-19 is trying to destroy the human race."

"It is! This is going to be a monumental test of our humanity. We are at war on so many fronts – with the disease itself, within our own society, within our own minds. We're fighting against the onslaught of poverty, radical changes in the way we live, the deterioration of our mental health, the destruction and erosion of what we had. Who we are is being redefined," he went on.

"I believe we can and will defeat the virus on a physical level through medication and vaccines; I have no doubt about that. Humanity will suffer a massive blow, but we will carry on and life will get better. It's just going to take some time, patience, fortitude, focus and, most importantly, kindness and cooperation.

"It's the spiritual fight within ourselves and our societies – the fear, anger, hatred, animosity I see spreading, which might be as insidious as the virus itself. These emotions are within us and are invisible —mentally, emotionally and spiritually."

"That's almost more deadly. There's no vaccine for it," I said.

"What's the antidote? Just love...or at least a level of respect for each other as fellow travelers on this planet. Without that, what do we have left?" he exclaimed.

"Chaos? War?" I replied.

"I hope not. Trust me, you don't want that. Look, right now everything is negative. We are experiencing radical shifts in our lives, living in a new reality with new rules, new priorities – masks, social distancing, washing hands incessantly, work from home, stay home as much as possible. Everything is shutting down. These radical shifts in our lives are going to require us to change our priorities both individually and collectively as a society.

"There are a few things that are imperative right now. The first one is to stay calm. Panic and fear are the normal visceral initial responses. They don't help. When you're in a state of fear or anxiety, you can't make proper decisions.

"Are you still meditating every day the way I taught you?" he asked suddenly.

"I...uh, well sometimes," I stammered.

"I'll take that as a No," Freddie replied unfazed. "Do you have a napkin?"

"I always do," I answered.

"Write across the top:

THE POWER OF TEN

"OK," I replied, not sure where Freddie was going with this but trusting he had a purpose.

"Under it write:

MEDITATE TEN MINUTES DAILY

"Meditation has been of paramount importance in helping me overcome my PTSD and calm my mind. I can't say enough about it. During this time of stress and uncertainty, your mental health and a positive state of mind are critical to getting through this.

"Second: stay healthy. Your mental and physical health must be your highest priority because we know, with Covid-19, a weakened immune system makes you susceptible to an attack by the virus. Keep your diet as healthy as possible and make sure you are exercising every day.

"Now write:

TEN HOURS A WEEK

"You should commit at least ten hours a week to exercise. It's the most important thing you can do right now.

"Third: adopt the attitude of victory at all costs. When the Germans were bombing England into oblivion during World War II, Winston Churchill declared during Britain's darkest hour: 'You ask, what is our aim? I can answer in one word: Victory. Victory at all costs – victory in spite of all terror – victory, however long and hard the road may be, for without victory there is no survival.' It's the win at all costs attitude you need to have; we need to have. There is no other option."

"You always have options – isn't that what you've told me," I tried to joke with Freddie.

"Yeah well, the other options are not good ones – I can tell you that. Our attitudes, perspectives and actions – not the virus, not the economy, not the election, none of them – are what we can utilize and control in the moment to change our circumstances. If we focus on these, we can not only survive but thrive through this pandemic. We cannot allow fear, worry, anger, doubt or any other negative emotions to find their way into and take over our conscious thinking.

"Next write down:

TEN MINUTE VISUALIZATION

"By creating in your mind a new image of what you want your future to look like, going forward, it will help with your motivation to stay focused. Remember, positive emotions must be cultivated; otherwise the negative emotions will dominate your thinking.

"Fourth: analyze the situation, assess your options and make the necessary adjustments based on the new information. Always start from the position that there is a way out, that there is a solution, a better way, even if you can't see it now. With that belief your mind will start looking for ways to find answers. You've lost your job, lost your apartment, you're living on a boat and Hollywood is closed. This new reality requires new skill sets, new attitudes, resilience, patience. It requires you to take new and different actions to recreate your life. Start thinking outside the box for new and different answers.

"Next write down:

SPEND TEN MINUTES EVERYDAY BRAINSTORMING

"The screenwriting career is on hold now; what are ten other ways you can make money writing? If you take ten minutes every day brainstorming ten new things you can do to better your position, you'll be amazed at what your mind comes up with. Maybe ten new ideas to write about, spend ten minutes talking to someone in a field you want to get into, whatever it is."

"That sounds like a lot of work," I whined.

"Oh, I see. Now under spend ten minutes everyday brainstorming write:

ANYONE CAN DO ANYTHING FOR TEN MINUTES!

"Yeah that's kind of true," I laughed.

"Remember, Chris, no masks, no crutches, no excuses. We are in a war…on many fronts…don't allow yourself to falter. Ten minutes every day compounded over the course of a month is roughly four hours of new and creative ideas that can lead you to the next level. Over the course of a year, you can make massive improvements and changes in your life.

Fifth: take massive daily action. It's easy to succumb to darkness and let it overtake us. We start feeling sorry for ourselves and let fear dominate our actions. You need to start working again and planning what your next move is going to be, assuming Hollywood stays closed for who knows how long. We don't know.

"I've been sending out resumes like crazy, I'm not getting any bites," I replied.

"You need to develop a Plan B for your life right now given the circumstances. Write out:

TEN HOURS A WEEK LEARNING A NEW SKILL

"Pick one thing, I don't care what it is, and spend ten hours a week learning a new skill that you want to have in your life. Maybe it's learning programming; maybe it's learning Spanish – I don't know. You'll probably find some ideas within your brainstorming sessions; but start working on a plan B for your next move. It will keep your mind focused on getting into the next chapter of your life. If you sit around and wait, your mind will start playing games with you. Now is not the time to allow stagnation to set in.

"Sixth: help others. Don't forget, Chris: God's currency is kindness. The more you invest in others, the more it comes back to you."

"You keep emphasizing focusing on others? My life is falling apart. I need to focus on myself," I retorted.

"Classic mistake I made. The reason I survived the war was that every soldier on the ship considered everyone else before himself. I am talking to you today because my friend and crewmate saved me from drowning and stepped in the way of enemy fire that would have killed me. He put me first.

"When I started my life in Dallas, I became obsessed with creating a fortune and I did. Nothing wrong with that, but in my pursuit, I neglected my family which was and is the most important priority in my life. I lost sight of that. I wasn't there for them and it cost me everything.

"I'm just saying, by focusing on others and helping them with their needs, it takes your focus off yourself. That 'focus' is a special power we all have. Even if it's for a brief moment, it can provide relief from your own thoughts that are tearing you down. Besides, I am convinced it is the only way we are going to get through this trying time. If everyone is at least considerate of others and we go through our lives mindful of those around us, willing to lend a helping hand when and where we can, we'll make it through to the other side victorious. If we don't, we're in big trouble.

"So next write out:

TEN THINGS YOU CAN DO TO HELP OTHERS

"Even if it's small things like smiling at the cashier, saying hello to people passing by or whatever comes to your mind, put the practice in motion. Think about this: what if we acted as if what we put out the energy into the universe – or God or whatever you want to call it comes back in some way twenty times greater?

"Does it?" I asked.

"I don't know the exact amount but I do believe what we put out comes back amplified. Why not believe it? What is wrong with that belief? I bet you would act a lot more compassionate in your day-to-day life if you acted according to that belief.

"Sounds like a good return on investment," I said.

"That's the point. So when you're having negative feelings and feeling sorry for yourself, reach out and help someone else.

"Put that into practice in your life. Do small things daily and over time, one foot in front of the other, and you will get to where you want to be. I know it's difficult, but it's doable. You just have to accept the fact that it's going to be challenging in the near future and you are going to be uncomfortable for a while."

"Gotta get comfortable being uncomfortable?" I asked.

"Now you're getting it!" Freddie chuckled.

Chapter Twenty-Two

FLEETING AS THE WIND

> Money is only a tool. It will take you wherever you wish, but it will not replace you as the driver.
>
> ~ *Ayn Rand*

I was feeling like a shipwrecked boat. Stuck in the marina, virtually no human contact, and barely any money in the bank... alone. The economy was collapsing, the virus was ripping through society decimating everyone and everything. I couldn't make sense of the chaos. Freddie was a lifeline, a lifeboat floating by in the middle of the ocean and I was drowning. Time to reach out again and grab the help I desperately needed.

"Hey Freddie, how are things in Texas?"

"Probably the same as California. Everything is upside down and inside out. Craziness, Chris! It's gotten way worse since we last spoke," he said.

"I'm getting really worried about money, Freddie. Things are really tight. I can't stop obsessing about it. It's becoming unhealthy," I said.

"We are in something completely different, totally unique in our history. Millions are out of work; businesses are shutting at a pace that is almost inconceivable. What can you do about it?" he asked me.

"I don't know."

"It looks like what you're doing about it is worrying about what you have no control over."

"I'm just afraid I'm not going to have enough to survive," I confessed.

"Fear is a natural reaction to what is happening," he said.

"Which is normal," I shot back.

"Of course it is – but is it effective?" he asked.

"Not really; it's just dominating my emotions."

"Do you have enough money now today? Are your needs being met today? Food in the fridge, roof over your head, health, people in your life who care about you?"

"Yes," I answered after a pause.

"That's all you have, Chris – right here right now. Everything else is a story you are telling yourself about the future. You are projecting into the future that there isn't going to be enough money. You're operating out of fear. No one knows what is going to happen. Is the virus going to mutate into something worse? Will a vaccine be created in 2021 that completely eliminates it and everything goes back to normal? I don't know. You don't know. All you have is right here, right now, and the power to control your perspective, attitude and actions. Everything else is out of your control.

He paused for a while and said, "Do me a favor, go outside your boat and try to stop the waves of the ocean."

"Obviously I can't; that's ridiculous, Freddie," I answered.

"What about the wind – can you stop it?" he asked.

"Of course not," I replied.

"Go stare at the sun," he commanded.

"I can't – you know that."

"I am pointing out the obvious, Chris. You're obsessing over the fear of things outside your control is as ridiculous as controlling the wind and the waves. The economy is going to do what it does. So is the virus. So is the government. We are in a storm and you are complaining about the winds, rain and tides crashing on your boat and you're afraid of them," Freddie went on.

"It's going to be hard; it just seems so bleak," I continued to lament.

"It is hard, damn hard, but it's in these times when you have to dig deep within yourself to recreate your life. Focus on what's in front of you right now. Remember we spoke about priorities?"

"Yes, we did."

"Money is obviously a priority in our lives, but it is, as we talked about, only one of the many priorities we are juggling. Trust me, at different times in your life, money takes on different meanings.

"When I was in Vietnam, I wasn't thinking about making money; I was thinking about how to not get shot and get out alive! Money wasn't much of a priority then – in fact, it had almost no priority. There were days that were so brutal I would have given a thousand dollars, if I had it, for a cold beer and a warm bed. The support and brotherhood of my fellow soldiers who were on the boat with me were much more important than money to me at that particular moment in my life.

"Having a lot of money doesn't necessarily mean you're going to be happy. I wasn't. When I built my clothing empire and owned real estate all over Dallas I neglected what was truly precious to me. Was it worth it losing my family, my marriage, my health and everything that had so much value in my life? It wasn't, trust me.

"In the aftermath of my Dallas downfall, I had the opportunity to create a new life, a better life. After I lost everything, I rebuilt my business in New York. It was a fraction of what I had before, just me and one assistant; but I was happy with that. I was now free to become who I truly wanted to become. Don't get me wrong, I still regretted losing everything at the time I had all those things, but I was able to heal myself from the PTSD and the depression that was tormenting me. I got sober and got my family back. Was it worth it? Absolutely!

"My life changed as I sought balance. Money wasn't controlling me; I was controlling it. That's a beautiful place to get to and what you should be striving for – balancing all the areas of your life equally and not letting one particular priority get out of hand putting you in a state of disequilibrium."

"At what point do you have enough money?" I asked.

"That's something you have to come to terms with, what you're comfortable with. Money is a tricky thing; it's what we as a society agree upon as a tool to conduct trade and exchange goods and services so we don't have to barter. See it as it is: a tool. The trap is not to let it control you. Don't let society dictate to you what you should do with your life in regard to money.

"For me, my serenity is preeminent. I know plenty of people who are extremely wealthy and extremely miserable. Some people never have enough; they're constantly keeping up with the Joneses. That is something you have to ask yourself. Are you comparing yourself to others and their level of wealth and what they have, compared to what you have? That's almost a guaranteed method that leads to disappointment and regret.

"There will always be someone with more money than you. That's just a fact. So, if you wanted to, you could create chronic misery in your life by comparing yourself to Elon Musk or someone wealthier than you and demoralize yourself about how you have failed in life. That option is always there for you if you want it, or you could take inventory of what is great in your life in spite of the loss, in spite of the pandemic, in spite of the economy.

"You think a brand-new sports car would make you happier? You've had the experience of building up expectations of buying new things and how you will feel once you acquire them. Does the feeling last?" Freddie asked.

"Not usually too long," I answered.

"That's the whole point. The major goal of advertisers is to have you feel miserable about your current state of existence – whatever that may be – and create an illusion in your mind that if you buy their products you will feel better about yourself. It's a lie. Now you have these projections on social media and television of this glamorous lifestyle. They are just brainwashing us to think that, if we had more money or had lives like the rich and famous, then we would be happy. It's a lie. We are chasing fantasies. If you pin your self-worth or happiness on your net worth, life is going to be very difficult because money can be as precarious as the wind.

"Money is a part of the cycle of existence we are talking about. Yes, you need it to exist in society and you have to work for it, but when does it become your master?

"The real value is your time, your health, and connections with those you care about and who care about you. These are finite resources. Your time with your loved ones here on the planet is limited. You can never get it back when it's gone. Governments can and will print more money and you can always earn more money, but you can't get more time back. Ever.

"Money comes and money goes, Chris. You know yourself that, even when you have a lot of money, it can be gone in an instant. My brother Lloyd is unable to move. He's dying in bed. Do you think he wouldn't give every penny he has to be cured and get his health back even for just one day?"

"I know I would," I said.

"Remember the homework assignment when you went to the graveyard?" he asked.

"How could I forget?" I said.

"Do you remember who the richest man in the graveyard was?" he asked.

"No," I answered.

"That's the whole point: it doesn't matter. You can't take it with you. I'm not saying not to build your empire; if that's what you want to do, go for it. Just take the time to be in the world with what is around you and who is around you and don't lose sight of what is truly valuable in life.

"Napkin time…you ready?"

"Of course, I've learned to be prepared for my homework," I told him.

"I'm sure during this time there are plenty of homeless people around the marina, right?"

"Tons. People living in tents everywhere. It seems to be getting worse by the day over on Venice Boulevard," I told him sadly.

"Go buy dinner for a homeless person. Just go out and get something once a month for someone less fortunate – and make it a habit. Once a month, buy them a meal or give them some food. It will help you get out of yourself when you put your focus on helping others. Again, it's an action to counteract the fear. It lets your mind know that there is abundance in your life and you're not afraid of not having enough."

"I can do that," I told him enthusiastically as we closed.

I knew a fantastic authentic Mexican restaurant right off Venice Boulevard and the next day on my morning walk I picked up some delicious tacos for some complete strangers. As usual, Freddie was right; they couldn't have been more grateful, and I had one of my best days ever on the marina.

Chapter Twenty-Three

ACKNOWLEDGE YOUR MISTAKES, FORGIVE YOURSELF

> I see it all perfectly; there are two possible situations—one can do either this or that. My honest opinion and my friendly advice is this: do it or do not do it—you will regret both.
>
> ~ *Søren Kierkegaard*

I was starting to regret my decision to move to California and pursue my dream of becoming a screenwriter. I blew through most of my life savings and was hanging on to an unemployment lifeline from the government. Living on the sailboat had been wonderfully peaceful for the first few months, but the madness was beginning to creep in.

I had way too much time alone. Due to Covid, everything was closed and there really was nowhere to go. I was spending countless hours by myself ruminating on my life choices and how I wound up here walking the Venice boardwalk and Santa Monica pier for hours on end. The beaches were desolate except for the army of police preventing anyone from congregating. It was surreal.

The "what if's" of my life were haunting me. I had plenty of time to mourn the past decisions I did and didn't make, money I wasted, opportunities I didn't take or took and didn't work out so well, things I said or didn't say or should have said, failed relationships.

I called Freddie to check on how he was doing. He was, as usual, in a great mood.

"How ya doin, Chris?"

"Not much has changed since the last Friday we talked. Just starting to lose my mind that's all," I said.

"You're spending too much time on the boat alone," he replied.

"There's nowhere to go, nothing to do," I said helplessly. "I'm really starting to regret my life and my decision to move out here. I should have stayed in New York in the computer field. I'd have a lot more money now," I told him. "I wouldn't be stuck on a boat watching the world collapse around me."

Freddie laughed knowingly. "Time alone will do that to you. Trust me; you're not the only one. A lot of people are feeling like you are now; it's normal. When life slows down like it has, we have so much time to reflect on what has been our life, up until now," he answered wisely.

"I'm torturing myself over what could have been, thinking about all the mistakes I've made," I told him.

"Ahhh, the Shoulda, Woulda, Coulda syndrome. We all experience it, and the older you get, _the more_ you'll experience it – trust me. I have more regrets than most humans are allowed to have.

"You want to talk about regrets? How often do I think, 'What if...?' I would have spent more time with my daughter – would her life be different? Could I have altered her future? Could I have prevented her from getting addicted to heroin? I would play endless scenarios in my mind. 'What if' I had steered the boat in a different direction? I wouldn't have hit the sandbar and fallen out of the boat. My friend O'Reilly would still be alive. You want to talk about regrets? I think I told you, at one point I had a net worth of over $20 million. I owned commercial real estate all over Dallas and wound up losing everything – my family, my business, my whole life, getting divorced and declaring bankruptcy. Everything was gone!

"The truth is we are human; we make mistakes. You tell yourself you did the best you could with the information you had at the time. We make decisions based on emotion, which often distorts our decision-making abilities," he confessed.

I could hear Freddie's voice starting to crack over the phone. He still had conflicting feelings around so many events and decisions that occurred in his life. I regretted bringing up the subject of regrets with Freddie. I knew it was opening old wounds that were painful for him to relive. There was a long pause in the conversation. I could tell he was gathering himself on the other side of the phone.

"The key is to forgive yourself, Chris," he said quietly. "It's not uncommon for us to torture ourselves with the 'what if's' of life. Just living on the planet you are going to have regrets – it's inevitable and impossible not to. If you have children, invariably there are going to be regrets. If you spend money or don't spend money there are going to be regrets. If you're in a relationship, you're going to have regrets about things you said or didn't say, things you did or didn't do. You'll have career regrets more than likely."

"Ya know, Freddie, my regrets aren't even close to what yours are, so I apologize for whining," I told him apologetically.

"No, Chris, they are real to you – they have real emotional impacts on your psyche. The reality is, we're always going to have regrets; it's how you deal with them. You make decisions and they bring you to points in your life. Sometimes they work out the way we want them to, but more often than not, they don't.

"The problem is too often we weave a story we sell to ourselves – like you are doing right now. You're saying to yourself, 'Had I stayed in New York and stayed in the computer business I would have this or that, or things would be different in my life.' It's self-deception. At the time you were feeling a certain way about your life and what was going on at the time, and you decided to make a change. I remember us going through your thought process and feelings twelve years ago when you wanted to leave your situation and pursue your passion. Now you're regretting it. At that particular time in your life, it's what you wanted to do. Now you are looking at it with remorse because things didn't work out the way you wanted them to.

"Those 'what if's' are endless...literally. There are thousands, tens of thousands of options that could have happened...but didn't. Tens of thousands of paths you could have taken...but didn't. There was only the one path – the one you took. The one I took. Here we are. We have to deal with what is in front of us now.

"It's OK to look back into the past...but don't stare. The key is to learn from your past – we all have one, many full of mistakes and regrets. Accept the fact that it won't matter in a thousand years and forgive yourself.

"One of the best ways to learn from the past, in particular, the regrets we have experienced, is to acknowledge them on paper. Once we have them written down in front of us, oftentimes the sting of the regret loses its power, or at least some of it. It makes it easier to see it from different angles.

"Have you ever heard of the poem *Six Serving Men* by Rudyard Kipling?" he asked suddenly.

"No," I replied.

"It goes something like this:

I KEEP six honest serving-men
They taught me all I knew
Their names are What and Why and When
And How and Where and Who.
I send them over land and sea,
I send them east and west;
But after they have worked for me,

I give them all a rest.

"It goes on for more, but I don't know the rest. You can check it on the internet if you want. The point of the poem is to look at things in your life with the six questions...what, why, when, how, where and who. Sounds simple, but I have found when dealing with regrets they are invaluable.

"I discovered this technique when I started working with my therapist in the Veteran Authority Hospital dealing with the trauma of PTSD surrounding the death of my best friend O'Reilly on that river boat in Vietnam. I just couldn't escape the guilt and remorse. For years it haunted me. It wasn't until I wrote down in detail what happened, why it happened, and worked through my feelings around the incident that I was able to free myself from the devastating emotions I was experiencing. The reality was we were in a war – it was total chaos – and things happen tragically. I was finally able to forgive myself.

"You have a pen with you?" Freddie asked.

"Of course, I never forget to have a pen and a napkin before we talk. I learned my lesson," I said. We both laughed.

"I want you to write out the event or decision or whatever you are having regret over at the top of the napkin. You said you were having regrets about moving to California to pursue a screenwriting career and leaving the computer business. Right?"

"Yes."

"OK, so write that down across the top of the napkin," he told me. "What happened and what are you feeling and why? Who is affected? What are you feeling about that? Where were you when you made the decision? Well, as I remember you were living in New York City and living and working with your ex-fiancée and you were miserable. When did you make the decision? After she moved to Switzerland and you'd had enough uncertainty. Why did you make the decision? You were terribly unhappy, remember? We were meeting every Friday to process what was going on in your life at the time. How did you come to the decision? We worked through it together to help you see a better future life for yourself. You felt you would have more money, you would have more happiness; you thought it would be a fulfilling career.

"You left for a better life. We get into trouble when we start making judgments about the decisions we make in our lives. They could be good or bad. The judgment we bring to it causes dissonance in our minds. The reality is what happened...happened. You made the best decision you could with the information you had at the time. See it for what it is - an event in your life. Try not to attach judgment to it.

"Another benefit of writing down the regret and the feelings around it and analyzing them from a distance on paper is you can see your role and mistakes in the event. When I lost everything in Dallas, I was drinking to deal with my PTSD. I'm not making any excuses; I just didn't know what was happening and it was the only way I knew how to deal with my trauma. By writing it out I could see how destructive my drinking was and I was able to change that behavior, knowing how dangerous it was not only to myself but to my family as well.

"We can accept responsibility for what happened, right the wrongs and make changes, going forward. Regrets can have a powerful impact on us to change the behavior that might have caused the regret or decision-making process, so make amends where necessary, learn from our mistakes and embrace what is great in our lives...today...now.

"Remember, we talked about the concept of time so many years ago? How little we have of it and how precious it is! Turn the focus of your mind on today because that is ultimately all you have anyway. Make it a masterpiece. Bring back into focus what is great in your life. This is the only life you have. Love it for what it is, for what you have, knowing it will not last forever. You can't go back in time, only forward. Why not go forward into your future free? Focus not on 'what if,' rather on 'what could be,' and work toward that future. Now enjoy your time on the boat. It won't last forever and focus on the next beautiful sunset."

Chapter Twenty-Four

THE VIEW WITH FRESH EYES

Everything has beauty, but not everyone sees it.

~ *Confucius*

"Focus on the next sunset. Focus on next sunset. Focus on the next sunset," I kept telling myself over and over, taking Freddie's words to heart and centering my attention on the beauty around me. The magic of the marina was beginning to wash over my consciousness – the weather, the waves, the smell of the ocean, the magnificent sunrises and sunsets. I didn't know God could paint with such majesty.

Everything was alive. The sea lions, the birds and all the other animals of the marina had no idea of Covid-19 or the economic catastrophe we were experiencing. They were oblivious to it, enjoying and living their lives in the splendor of the waterfront.

Immersing myself in the ways of the Marina was helping me liberate my mind to some degree. I tried to lose myself in the wonder of it all in between frantically and frenetically emailing my resume to find work. All the animals of the marina were constantly hunting for food and I was hunting for a job. I guess we did have something in common besides living together.

I had to occupy my mind with something constructive, so I started rewriting my screenplays and turning them into novels. Because everything was closed, I would sit at the beach most of the time totally alone and watch the seagulls and birds I had never seen before play like children in the water. I had to look up their names – herons, egrets, willets, marbled godwits, cormorants, to name a few. They all sounded like characters out of a Harry Potter book and they were equally as magical. I watched as the pelicans hovered above the water and suddenly plunged into the ocean from a hundred feet in the air, coming up after a few seconds underwater with a mouthful of fish.

The harbor took on a life of its own, distracting me from the outside world. Covid-19, the election and the economy were the only things dominating the news…so I got rid of my TV. Since television was introduced to me at the age of five, I don't think I was ever without a TV in my life. I was living on the boat and nature became my television. I just didn't want to deal with the electronic noise and distractions. Most of it, if not all of it, was out of my hands anyway. What I could control was what I chose to focus on, so I spent countless hours watching the water spellbound by the mystery of it all. Where we came from and where we are going all comes back to the water in one form or another.

I was starting to feel a "shift" take place, so I figured it was time to call Freddie.

"Yo Freddie, how are you holding up in the new Covid world?"

"Same old sixes and sevens. Everything is shut down but I›m holding my own. How about you?" he replied.

"Just spending as much time as I can with my seagull buddies and getting lost walking the beach. I don't know what else I can do. Everything is closed here as well. Such crazy times, huh Freddie?"

"You've heard the expression: "Everything changes but change itself?"

"Yeah, I guess that's true."

"America as I once knew it for the last seventy-two years is gone. My life as I once knew it is gone. Your life is now different than it once was, and probably will never be the same," he sighed.

"Life has changed. We're in a new reality now," I said.

"Or is it just the same reality in just a different time? You know, we've had pandemics throughout history. It's just been a hundred years since the last one that's all. Prior generations have experienced pandemics - now it's our turn. Every generation thinks theirs is unique, somehow different and new. I guess it's new to them as to us, but pandemics, tumultuous wars, political unrest and upheaval have been with us since the beginning of civilization. Like I've always said, you have to adapt to the times and circumstances the way they are now, not the way they used to be or the way you want them to be," he expounded.

I thought about what Freddie was saying. "Why should I be surprised this was happening? I was on the Planet Earth experiencing history unfold as it would without regards to my feelings, opinions or desires. I realized I was going to have to change and accept the new normal – wearing a mask everywhere, social distancing, strange human behavior, economic abnormality, lockdowns, incessant washing of my hands. Eating out at a restaurant was becoming a thing of the past. Life was very different, and I wasn't sure if or when it would ever change back.

"Enjoy the marina while you have it, Chris. As I've told you so many times before, nothing lasts forever. Hold onto those moments you are having now. In spite of the turmoil happening around us, there is still beauty. We often fail to realize the wonder of life until it has passed us by.

"I remember a very specific moment I had on the Mekong River Delta. I couldn't sleep all night, so I figured it was easier to just stay awake. The entire boat crew was sleeping. It was just me in the Universe alone. The sun was rising and there was an indescribable calmness on the water except for the occasional fish jumping and splashing around. The orchestra of sounds echoed from the jungle across the river as the sun started to peek above the canopy of the trees. Out of nowhere, a giant bird, its wingspan had to be seven feet, if not longer, swooped down over the boat. It looked like a flying dinosaur with yellow and red feathers and an orange beak that had to be a foot long. As it passed overhead it made a howling screech proclaiming its majesty and dominance over the jungle. It felt like I was in a dream.

"At that moment I had a profound revelation. Everything in the Universe seemed to make sense: there was a rationality and perfectness to it all. In spite of the horrors of the war, I had an instant knowing that God was real, and that the Earth was composed perfectly in its own way. The bird gracefully soared into the jungle and I sat back and watched in awe as it all unfolded before me. The beauty and mystery of the Universe were always right there in front of me, I was just lost in the hell that was the war and couldn't experience it.

"Things are bleak now, that's exactly why we need to see past the darkness and revel in the beauty of the world - music, art, love, romance, the human creative spirit. Think what a privilege it is to be on the planet at this time now in history in spite of whatever is going on. I know hundreds of guys who aren't so lucky.

"If people spent more time watching the sunset, actually planning it into their daily routines, their lives would be orders of magnitude better. When I was living in Hawaii with my girlfriend, we had a ritual every night where we would watch the sunset and reflect on the beauty that was in our lives. We would talk to each other about everything good, everything great, everything miraculous, and what a privilege it was having each other and those moments we had together.

"I need to get back to that practice – thanks for reminding me. No matter what is happening in my life, and we both know things will happen, I can allocate fifteen minutes to watch the sunset every night.

"Want some homework?" Freddie asked.

"I got my napkin ready," I said. We both laughed as usual.

"You don't need a napkin, just your phone. You have a camera on it right?

"Yup."

"Take some photos of some sunsets. Get up early a couple of days and get some photos of the sunrise, snap some shots of some birds, of the beach. Capture the beauty around you with your camera. You can start documenting your time on the boat. It's important to take those few moments every day to reflect with gratitude on what's great in your life. Trust me, when you're my age looking back on your time on the boat, it will all seem like a dream. At least you'll have the photos to remind you of how lucky you were to have that experience even in the face of what was going on in the world around you."

"Now that's homework I will actually like doing," I told him. It was good to hear Freddie's laugh across the phone.

Chapter Twenty-Five

RHYTHMS AND CYCLES

> All human life has its seasons and cycles, and no one's personal chaos can be permanent. Winter after all gives way to spring and summer, though sometimes when branches stay dark and the earth cracks with ice, one thinks they will never come, that spring, and that summer, but they do, and always.
>
> ~*Truman Capote*

It was Friday again and the Covid crisis was escalating rapidly. Breakouts everywhere. Panic rifling through the markets and populations all over the world. No one knew what was going on or how to deal with this strange virus that was ripping the country apart.

I was on my boat eating canned tuna which I had waited in line for hours at Costco, not knowing like everyone else what was going to happen next. Would it be like the Spanish flu killing 50 million people around the world? What would happen to the economy? Hollywood was shut down totally.

Freddie didn't seem to be too bothered when I spoke to him on the phone. "Funny, you don't think you're part of history until it happens to you. Then you're in it. It's easy to look at it from a distance in a history book; but experiencing it in your own life is a whole different ball game. It's a normal part of life; we just don't like it when it does. I'm not minimizing the pain and suffering involved in it all, trust me, but it's here now – what are we going to do about it? What is going to be our perspective towards it? Are we going to react in fear and worry or respond with calculated calm methodical planning and effort?" he asked.

"What do you think, Freddie? What is going to happen?" I asked him.

"I have no idea, but I have faith we'll figure it out. We've been here before, not in our lifetime, but humanity has faced plagues like these in past generations and we got through them."

"But what if this time it's different? What if this is the one that sinks the human race?" I asked unsure if I really wanted the answer.

"We are going through what I call a horseshoe moment," Freddie stated.

"A horseshoe moment?"

"Yes, at one point in our history not too long ago, people were making horseshoes for horses, and probably were doing pretty well. Then one day out of nowhere a model T Ford sputtered by their horseshoe store – and it was the beginning and the end. The beginning of a new era in automobiles and, by and large, the end of the horseshoe guys and probably the saddle maker guys as well. Covid-19 might just be our modern-day horseshoe moment.

"These seismic shifts happen to us personally all the time: someone gets cancer, a loved one dies, you lose your job. It's just now happening to our society and the world. Our nation is facing the death of the life we once used to live – going to the movies, the freedom to move around without the fear of getting infected, going to an office to work. We are in a new and different cycle of our existence personally and collectively.

"It's all cycles, Chris – everything. Products, people, economies, nations, nature exist in cycles and we are in a particular part of a cycle at a particular time. What we often fail to realize is that our lives exist within the same framework of rhythms and seasons. Once you understand this, it's easier to accept the situation you are in.

"Become aware of the natural processes of life. You are in the winter, or a winter season at this part of your life. What happens in winter? It's cold, it snows, nature contracts, things die off, nature hibernates waiting for spring.

"Right now you're on a boat, collecting unemployment; Hollywood is shut down. These are the facts now. They will change. We know spring will come."

"It's just when is the question," I added.

"No one knows. Have to be patient in winter and hopeful for the coming spring. Use your time now to plan your crops, so to speak, for the coming season of your life," Freddie advised me.

"Kind of reminds me of the Frank Sinatra song, I can't remember it goes something about May and June...," I said.

Freddie didn't hesitate and started singing into the phone:

"That's life, that's what all the people say
You're riding high in April, shot down in May
But I know I'm gonna change that tune
When I'm back on top, back on top in June..."

We both laughed. Freddie reminded me of Frank Sinatra. He had that old school quality you don't find much anymore in people. His words were golden; he had a charm and charisma that he brought to others no matter who they were. Always with a cheerful word or smile, he knew that value of kindness and made sure to spread it around.

"I knew you'd know the song Freddie," I told him as I smiled into the phone.

"That's the whole point of the song, Chris: the cycles of life. It's called *Samsara*.

"*Samsara*?" I asked.

"It's what the ancient Buddhist and Hindu religions referred to as the inevitable cycles of birth, life and death that everything goes through. Things are constantly shifting, evolving, changing and they ultimately end for everyone and everything. Then a new cycle starts. That is the way of the world. Nothing we can do about it.

"I'm growing some tomatoes in my apartment now and one of my plants just died. The tomatoes started to bloom and for some reason died on the vine. I don't know why, I did everything I could to make it the healthiest plant possible, just nature in her ways had other plans. I could have run around my apartment telling myself what a failure I was, or what a horrible situation the plant was in and worry about the future of the rest of plants. Or I could step outside the circumstance with detached judgment and observe the process happening as it's supposed to," he explained.

"You should get a tomato plant, Chris, it'll change your outlook," he suggested.

"Why a tomato plant?" I asked.

"It's a great illustration of nature's cycles and our powerlessness as we watch as they unfold. My tomato plant is going through its own process as nature dictates in the same way you and everyone else are going through their own cycles of life.

"Remember my daughter who was struggling with addiction?" he asked.

"Yeah I do. How is she doing?" I asked.

"Well, she just relapsed on heroin again and is in rehab again. It kills me, Chris, I'm here for her and will do anything to help her, but the cycles of her life are unique to her experience. I must practice detachment from the outcome and allow her to go through her process as we all have to. All I can do is be there for her. Like the tomato plant, so many things are outside my ability to control.

"My brother Lloyd is dying in front of me – what can I do? I just spend as much time with him as I can and be grateful for the time we still have left together. Death is supposed to happen; it's the last cycle of our existence. I have to accept it as nature's way."

"That's heavy, Freddie, I'm sorry to hear that," I replied.

"Well, Chris, it is as the chairman of the board said," and Freddie started singing into the phone... "That's life that's what they say..." He broke out of his song ... "Seriously get yourself a tomato plant this week. It'll change your life if you let it. When your mind starts drifting, the tomato plant will be there to remind you of the process of *Samsara,* and accepting what's great about whatever cycle you are in."

Freddie had a certain wisdom about him. I was starting to understand why he saw things the way he did. He had been in and out of hell a few times, and his mission was to help others find their way out without asking for anything in return.

Another homework assignment from Freddie that I didn't quite understand, but I knew he only had my best interests at heart, and there was a lesson buried within whatever he was asking me to do.

"I'll get the tomato plant," I promised him.

Chapter Twenty-Six

MEMORIES

Remembering that I'll be dead soon is the most important tool I've ever encountered to help me make the big choices in life.

Almost everything--all external expectations, all pride, all fear of embarrassment or failure--these things just fall away in the face of death, leaving only what is truly important. Remembering that you are going to die is the best way I know to avoid the trap of thinking you have something to lose. You are already naked. There is no reason not to follow your heart.

No one wants to die. Even people who want to go to heaven don't want to die to get there. And yet, death is the destination we all share. No one has ever escaped it, and that is how it should be, because death is very likely the single best invention of life. It's life's change agent. It clears out the old to make way for the new.

~ Steve Jobs

I was beginning to come to terms with my new Covid reality. It was Friday, time to call Freddie. He was having some health issues, so I was a little concerned. I gave him a call around lunch time and left a message. He was two hours ahead of me in Texas and I knew he went to bed early, so I didn't want to call him too late. I texted him later in the evening to call me when he got a chance.

Saturday came and went; still no contact from Freddie. Sunday morning I called him as soon as I woke up. Nothing. Same thing Monday and Tuesday – no answer. Now I was really getting worried. He wasn't answering his emails or texts, and I didn't have his daughters' phone numbers, so there was nothing I could do. A few more days went by but still nothing.

Then I got a brief text from Freddie around midnight Sunday night. He apologized for not getting back to me and told me his brother Lloyd had fallen gravely ill. He had to fly out to New York to get some of Lloyd's affairs in order and would call me when he got back to town. I breathed a sigh of relief and texted him back wishing him the best.

His brother Lloyd had a terrible childhood and overcame enormous obstacles in his life. He was Freddie's closest friend and confidant. Lloyd was an active member of Alcoholics Anonymous and had over forty years clean and sober. He was a wonderful human being whom I had the honor of meeting several times while I was living in New York City.

Friday showed up quicker than usual, and Freddie called me early in the morning. I could tell from his voice something was wrong.

"Hey Chris, sorry I haven't gotten back to you. I've been off the grid for the past few days coping with Lloyd's death. Unfortunately, he passed away Wednesday night in his sleep in my apartment. At least he was able to spend the last few days of his life surrounded by the people who loved him," Freddie said.

I didn't know what to say. I knew Lloyd was sick and he was battling brain cancer, but I had no idea how bad it was. What do you say when someone's loved one dies? I just told him how I really felt.

"Sorry to hear that, Freddie. I met Lloyd a few times and he was really kind to me. I know you guys were really close," I said.

"He was a great guy, Chris. I've probably gotten thirty to forty phone calls from people he helped in AA in New York City telling me how much he impacted their lives and how much he gave back. Lloyd helped hundreds of people get sober and was the most giving person I ever knew."

"That's saying something about him. How are you holding up?" I asked.

"I knew this day was coming soon, but it still hurts. Lloyd and I have been best friends since we were young kids. We've been through so much together. Since he was a teenager, he's battled with Hepatitis C and was actually the longest living survivor with a liver transplant in New York City. The last few years of his life the brain cancer has been spreading, yet in spite of all his health issues, he kept fighting and kept helping people even until the last days of his life. That was his spirit."

"You're lucky he was your brother," I told him.

"I couldn't have asked for anyone better, Chris. I'll miss him."

I could hear Freddie over the phone trying to keep his composure.

"He was dealt a bad hand but turned it around. He's my hero."

"It's tough dealing with loss," I tried to reassure him.

"It's devastating. But it is the way of the world. The yin and yang of it all, life and death. We all go through it. Doesn't make it easier but, like I've told you before, Chris, accept life for what it is as it is. Death is supposed to happen. Nature is the boss, not me. I don't make the rules; she does. All we can do is try to keep death as far away from us as long as we can, but in the end, it is a debt we all must pay at some time in our not too distant future.

"Knowing that it will occur, your job is to make peace with death and what you believe happens after you die. Any way you slice it, the hard truth is that you will stop being on this planet at some point. You don't know when, although with every moment that passes, you are getting one step closer to that moment...*the moment.* It's the when and how that are the great mysteries," he said.

"And the where-are-we-going thing? That's kinda the big one too, right?" I remarked.

"That is kinda the big one. That's why it's important to work through your philosophy about what is next. Some believe in a heaven and hell, some in karma and returning to earth in different manifestations based on their deeds while they are here now. Some believe in nothingness: when we die it's lights out, nothing more. Some believe in different realms we potentially go to. I've read recently some believe we are actually living in a computer simulation. I don't know for sure what comes next. I can only work through what seems to make sense to me.

"When you take the time to work out within yourself and your experiences what you think happens when you die, then you will eliminate much of the fear around it. Once you accept it, and really accept it, and make peace with it, like I had to in the war, your life takes on a different meaning. You will gain a new sense of freedom. Your perception of time changes because you realize you have so little left. Relationships take on a deeper meaning because you know they won't last forever. You'll see them as the gift they truly are for the brief span of time you have them. You'll appreciate your health more knowing your body will one day deteriorate and you will get sick and you will die."

"Sounds a little morbid, Freddie," I told him.

"It's not morbid; it's reality. As the saying goes, "For whom the bell tolls, it tolls for thee." Like I told you before, many people don't start living their lives until it's too late. I was fortunate to come to terms with the reality of the transience of life at a young age. I've never forgotten that. That's why I do the ritual to keep it fresh in my mind.

"Chris, I just turned seventy-two and it all seems like a blur. I remember being five years old running around with Lloyd in

Queens like it was yesterday. The older I get, the faster time seems to go by."

"What ritual do you do?" I inquired.

"I set aside one day every month to reflect on the people I have loved and lost and the brevity of my own humanity. On the fourteenth of every month when I wake up and right before I go to sleep, I make a special tea my mother taught me how to brew. I use a porcelain teapot she used when I was a child and the teacups we used as kids. It's a kind of ceremony I do to remind myself of loved ones lost and how brief our time here on earth really is. It helps me center myself," he explained.

"Why the fourteenth?" I asked.

"October 14, 1986 was when my mother died. I find having a ritual keeps her memory alive and reminds me I'm not destined to live forever. My fate is the same as those I have known and loved in my life. One day I will join those who have left before me.

"You got your napkin and pen?" Freddie asked.

"I always do," I told him.

"Pick one day a month and do something in remembrance of those whom you have loved and lost. Find something that has meaning to you, or something you enjoy. Maybe put on your favorite song to bring about that feeling of connection you had when they were with you."

"So I can play the Rolling Stones and smoke my favorite Cuban cigar? Is that an acceptable ritual?" I asked.

"Whatever works for you, my friend; just make it an enjoyable experience. Remember those moments you spent with those you loved who have passed on. Reflect on how little time you really have left on the planet knowing *the moment* is coming and how each day it gets closer than the day before," Freddie said.

"I guess that's one way to light a fire underneath someone," I said.

"It's the ultimate truth: time is running out. Get doing what you need and want to before your fire is extinguished. No more whistling past the graveyard. Or do I need to send you back to the cemetery for some more homework?" Freddie asked.

"No, no, a good Cuban cigar and some Rolling Stones once a month while I watch the sunset is good enough for me," I replied.

"Oh! Speaking of sunsets, send me some pictures of the marina will ya? I need some cheering up."

"They're on their way. Talk to you next Friday."

"Oh, before you go, what is the Stones' song?" he asked.

"Waiting on a Friend," I answered.

"Good choice. I like it. Talk to you next week!" Freddie said.

Chapter Twenty-Seven

PRACTICE HIGHER SELF

> I wish that people who are conventionally supposed to love each other would say to each other, when they fight, 'Please — a little less love, and a little more common decency.'
>
> ~ *Kurt Vonnegut*

I developed a friendship with a couple of seagulls who kept me company when I got lonely. I made the mistake of feeding them a few times while sitting on my deck with my morning coffee, not realizing how intelligent they actually are. They would show up a few hours after sunrise and start squawking outside my boat, waking me up to feed them. If you've never heard a choir of seagulls, it can be quite the ruckus. Nature's alarm clock. As soon as I emerged from the cabin onto the deck, their chorus of squawks would get louder and louder as they eagerly awaited whatever I had on the menu for them that particular morning.

After a couple of weeks of my generosity, word must have gotten out in the bird community in the marina. My morning ritual of feeding only a few select seagulls was turning into a full-scale brawl. It wasn't just between the seagulls anymore, but a whole host of different species of birds I had never seen before started arriving en masse.

The birds of the marina seemed to have an affinity for ham more than any other food I fed them. The more ham I threw into the water, the more they wanted, and more birds appeared. It wasn't until the pelicans came along that the game for all the others was over. They were way bigger, much more ferocious and made sure everyone knew it.

It was Friday, time to call Freddie and tell him about the avian invasion at my boat. I called him in the middle of the feeding frenzy. I knew that would cheer him up.

"Hey Freddie, how ya feelin?" I asked him.

"I can barely hear you, Chris. What's that noise in the background?"

The squawks of the birds outside my boat were drowning out our conversation.

"It's the birds of the marina!" I shouted into the phone as I made my way back into the cabin closing the door behind me. "There are about thirty different birds outside my boat fighting for pieces of ham I'm tossing into the ocean. Three pelicans swooped in and are chasing all the other ones away. It's quite the sight."

Freddie laughed. "Send me some pictures."

I could see him smiling across the phone. That was what I was looking for. I told Freddie the background story about how I met the seagulls and the pelican incursion.

"Sounds like what's going on in our society. Everyone is fearful and selfish. They're afraid they aren't going to have enough, and we are feuding amongst ourselves. People getting into fights in line at the supermarket over toilet paper just like the birds fighting for pieces of ham. The tension between people is rising. I haven't seen this in the seventy-three years of my life.

"Society is starting to fragment at the seams – the riots, looting, cities being set on fire, everybody locked in their homes. The political parties are waging war for power to win the election, causing dissension in society. The energy is anger. What I worry about is the animosity that is growing, not just in America but globally. If we're not careful, it can morph into something we might lose control of," he explained.

"That's how it always happens," I replied.

"You're right. We must stop this crescendo of hate and anger before it's too late. Once that tension has escalated to a certain point, it is hard to turn back. All it takes is a little spark to ignite catastrophic outcomes," he warned.

"It's funny, Freddie, we're not that much different than the seagulls when you think about it. We're obsessed with ourselves," I observed.

"Like the birds on your boat, many people don't evolve out of thinking about themselves. All their actions revolve around getting what they want and need without any thought of others," he said.

"They're birds, they can't do anything but think about themselves," I replied.

"That's my point! As humans we can do something about our behavior. Unlike the seagulls, we can choose to evolve above our animal instincts, our self-centered impulses, and think of others despite the circumstances surrounding us, no matter how dire we may perceive them to be. We can practice altruism. They can't."

"How do we do that? How do we stop this descent into darkness?" I asked.

"We have to evolve spiritually. We can choose a higher frequency. Call it love, higher self, a higher energy – whatever you want to call it – that's what separates us from our animal counterparts. We can choose those higher vibrations of consciousness. All the great spiritual teachers throughout our short history on earth have taught that unconditional love is the guiding principle we should cultivate in our lives. It's the strongest force keeping us together.

"We're humans on this rock hurtling through space circling the sun at 67,000 miles per hour sharing this common experience called humanity on Planet Earth. We are all connected in some strange mystical way and all come from the same source, whatever it is. We are still trying to figure out the how and why of it all. Once we break away from that connection is when the judgment and disintegration begin. We must start loving each other, or...I don't know what's going to happen, but I can assure you it's nothing good," Freddie explained with a tone of sadness in his voice.

"What is love really? It's tossed around in songs and books – but what is it really? Sounds so nebulous," I asked.

"Life's great mystery, I guess. It is what philosophers, poets, and artists have been asking since the beginning of time. The word itself doesn't really do justice to what it represents. It's one of those words that can mean so many different things like the word car. What is it ultimately? A car is a vehicle to get you where you want to go, but when you break it down, it has many parts: transmission, braking system, cooling system, steering system and so forth.

"Love, in a similar fashion is like a car. It is a vehicle we use to create harmony with others while we are living together on the planet; yet it is somewhat more complicated in exactly what it is. Like a car, love has so many components: forgiveness, altruism, patience, acceptance, sacrifice, commitment. It takes the form of a feeling; however, the feeling often fades with time. Love ultimately is much more than a feeling. I believe it is energy and action.

"Often love dictates what you need to do even when you might not want to do it. When I lost everything in Dallas and my brother Lloyd let me live with him in New York for two years while I rebuilt my life, that wasn't a feeling. O'Reilly gave his life for me when he stepped in front of machine gun fire to save me. He was my brother; I would have done it for him too, no questions asked. That wasn't a feeling. There have been times when I've had to cut myself off completely from my daughter because of her heroin addiction. Sounds harsh, but I love her beyond anything else in my life and that action at that time was what I needed to do. Enabling her wasn't going to help her. That wasn't a feeling."

"It's easy to love those you care about, but what about people we don't know, like strangers we meet on the street? How do you love them?" I asked.

"That's true," he said. "We are constantly interacting with other people – children, parents, friends, spouses, siblings, strangers, neighbors, coworkers. Obviously, the level of intention and energy we give them depends on how well we know them, but regardless of who they are, the least we can do is have a certain level of commitment to civility and courtesy to everyone we come in contact with. Common courtesy, a thank you, excuse me, and I'm sorry go a long way in the world around us.

"This concept of love, if we simplify it, is basically thinking in terms of others just a little more in our daily lives. It is just being kind a little bit more and not reacting in anger at the first sign of conflict. It is about choosing our response to the event, rather than reacting. The more we practice it, the more it becomes a habit and part of who we are. At least we can try. It's all we can do," he explained.

"You're like Saint Freddie," I said. We both laughed.

"That I can assure you I am not. I just try to put it out there. It's really in the day-to- day living where we can implement the higher good.

"Listen, the other day I was walking down the street and I noticed a girl pulling out of her parking spot and she had left her coffee on the roof.

"She forgot it on the roof?" I asked incredulously.

"Yes, so I stopped her before she pulled out and took it off the roof and gave it to her. Her smile was priceless. I'm sure I made her day. The odds of her passing that energy on to the next person probably doubled."

"That's the idea, right?" I asked.

"That's it. So simple, it's almost childlike. If we do that we can't lose. It's like the old adage, "An apple a day keeps the doctor away. I don't really see a downside to eating an apple a day, neither do

I see a downside to being kind to strangers. I mean, wouldn't you want someone to grab your coffee off your roof and give it to you if you left it there? A nice tall cup of your favorite morning coffee, only to be spilled across your car and ruin your day?"

"Absolutely!" I answered.

"Little things like that, Chris, can be game changers in the lives of others. I always make it a point to say something kind to any person I come in contact with during the course of my day, whether it's the person at Starbucks, or the gas station attendant or if I'm standing in line waiting at the grocery store. It's just good karma if nothing else. "You've heard the adage: 'Do unto others as you would have them do unto you?'" he asked me.

"Of course," I replied.

"A pretty straightforward and simple concept, but if applied in our lives, it can revolutionize how we can live on the planet together. It's the ideal we should strive for. It's important not to forget the second part of the adage "do unto you." It's paramount to love yourself. We are all flawed; all have scars, mistakes, injustices done to us and we've done likewise to others. Gotta forgive ourselves; we are human we aren't robots. Part of the process of love is turning that energy on ourselves," Freddie explained.

"Seems kind of selfish," I replied.

"In a way it is, but you put a hook in the ocean to catch a fish to eat, right? Is that selfish? No, you have to feed yourself to live. In the same way you have to forgive yourself to live free from self-hatred, regret, guilt and remorse.

"Did I ever tell you a few years ago I went back to Vietnam?"

"No, did you go for a vacation?" I asked.

"No, I went back seeking forgiveness. I haven't told many people about it, but it's relevant to what we're talking about now. After everything fell apart in Texas and I moved back in with Lloyd in New York City, I did a lot of soul searching. Vietnam just kept coming up. I knew I had to go back and make amends for that time in my life. That's why I've constantly told you to put that energy out; it will come back to you."

"What did you do there?" I asked.

"Well, it was after I was starting to make money again in the garment business in New York and I had some money saved. I really didn't know what I was going to do, but I knew I had to go back and face my demons. Once I got there, I just started walking around some of the villages where we had been waging war and handed out money to the poorest people I could find. I didn't speak the language, so I just smiled...a universal language of its own. I did this for two weeks and flew back home to New York. I had to bring closure to that part of my life to get forgiveness. It was just part of my journey to heal myself. You don't have to make a trek halfway across the world to align yourself with the higher good and get forgiveness, or maybe you do, I don't know. You have to find the answer within yourself. Going back to Vietnam was just what I felt I needed to do.

"I've experienced so much negative energy in my life; I like the good stuff better, Chris. It just makes life easier and better. Remember we spoke about spiritual investment? I've told you so many times before, it comes back to you multiplied.

"My mother was a Buddhist and believed in karma and what we do here determines how we will come back in the next life. I don't know if it's true, but I try to live as if it's true. I don't want to come back as a cockroach in Manhattan and have someone squash me getting off the subway, all because I didn't practice kindness while I was here now in this body. Besides, what's the worst thing that could happen? You're gonna bring a smile to someone's face and brighten their day? Think about it. It's an absolute no-lose situation.

"Break out the napkin and write down two things. I'm borrowing this from Ben Franklin. He had this practice and it's helped me tremendously. When he woke up he asked himself the question: 'What good shall I do this day?' At the end of the day, he would answer the question: 'What good have I done today?' This is a good practice to get your mind thinking differently. I find it actually helps me to anticipate acts of kindness I might do in the day ahead.

"Next I want you to write out a kindness mantra," he said.

"What's that?" I asked.

"We were talking about loving strangers, or at least being kind to strangers, and I know at times it can be very difficult – someone cuts in front of you on the freeway, bumps into you at a grocery store. You know what I mean. A lot of people are suffering and not just because of the virus – far be it for me to judge what someone is going through in their life especially now. We all struggle at different times and might not always be in a great mood.

"I have developed a practice when I feel the temperature rising and there might be tension with someone. I stop, take a deep breath and I say to myself: "This is a triviality in life and a part of normal living. Nothing compares to my serenity. Practice higher self." You can use a common prayer, or you can create a mantra of your own. Make it personal to you. Memorize it and when you get into an uncomfortable situation with someone or even if you're alone feeling depressed or anxious. Pause, take a deep breath and repeat your mantra to yourself over and over. It will help you cultivate that serenity that we so desperately crave and need. It's a simple technique I use to help me stay centered.

"Next make a list of ten people you haven't talked to in years – old friends, relatives, people you used to know. Give them a call and catch up. Tell them what they mean to you. It will brighten their day, I promise. It's a simple practice to put into the universe the higher energy I was telling you about. Most importantly, like I told you before, put out kindness and it will come back to you multiplied. If we each helped each other, even if it's just a little bit every day in small ways, the cumulative efforts over time build a formidable life of compassion and generosity. One of the easiest ways to put positive energy into the universe is a simple phone call.

"Finally, as you go out in the world tomorrow morning just think to yourself, 'Hold the door for others.' It's a simple but effective way to evolve into your higher self and radiate love and kindness to those you will meet along your journey. If we all just thought along those lines of 'holding the door for others' and practiced that principle in our daily lives, we could transform the world around us for the better. I have no doubt about it.

"If we can agree on the beauty of the sunset, we can agree on how we are going to live together and treat each other," Freddie concluded.

As usual, I was in a different frame of mind after talking to Freddie and had a few months' worth of homework assignments to complete, but I knew what he was telling me would create profound changes in my thinking...if I did the work.

EPILOGUE

As usual, my conversations with Freddie were challenging and I noticed profound shifts in my thinking. My situation on the boat was manageable, and I was making the best of it, but Freddie wouldn't let me get away without working through my options.

"Extrapolate, Chris, extrapolate. Where is this going if you continue in this course of your life? You're on the boat, Hollywood is closed, unemployment will run out and what are you going to do for money?" Freddie would constantly ask me.

"I'm going to be 51 soon and I've done so much. I really don't want to go back to where I was. I just don't think it would be fulfilling or interesting," I told him.

"Have you ever thought of getting on the road? Seeing our great majestic countryside?" Freddie asked.

"The thought never really entered my mind, I really don't want to give up my dream of writing," I said.

"You don't have to. Listen a lot of great writers spent time on the road - Jack Kerouac, John Steinbeck, Bukowski, F. Scott Fitzgerald, and Hunter S. Thompson, to name a few. It will change your perspectives, I'm sure of that.

"I spent a lot of time on the road when I was building my company, traveling all over the states. It's a wonderful country and it's worth seeing. Especially now might be great time for you to do it. You can get out, see the world, you'll save some money, and I'm sure you'll get new material for writing. It'll do you good to get out of LA and off the boat while the pandemic keeps raging on. There's a great big country out there: it's time you saw it!" he recommended.

I had to think about it seriously. I'd never spent much time outside the two major cities, New York and Los Angeles. The thought of roaming the countryside had a romantic appeal, and it made sense economically. After all, I was fifty and money was tight. Who knew when Hollywood would open up again? I just couldn't go back to the corporate world. Freddie made a great point about several of my literary heroes who had spent time on the open road and wrote some of America's literary masterpieces. I thought about the good, the bad and the ugly scenarios surrounding that option as a career. LA wasn't going anywhere. I could always go back to my life there. Besides, if those legendary writers were willing to do it, there was no reason I couldn't or shouldn't.

I got in touch with a department within Los Angeles County, which had a program where they would train me to get my commercial driver license. My dream of becoming a successful writer might take on a new dimension once I got "on the road." Like Freddie always told me, "You never know what is around the next corner of your life. You just need to have the courage to make the changes." I was so used to computers and offices, the trucking industry opened up a whole new world to me.

I passed my test, got trained by an over-the-road carrier, and hit the pavement roaming the United States hauling freight to areas of the country I couldn't have imagined existed and meeting people from all walks of life. The stories are endless and fascinating.

One thing has been constant. Freddie and I still speak every Friday and the lessons he teaches me have even more importance and precedence than ever before as I navigate the concrete seas of this great land.

DEDICATION

This book is dedicated to Lloyd Clemett,
a quiet, kind hero in the face
overwhelming adversity.

AUTHOR'S NOTE

When you arise in the morning think of what a privilege it is to be alive, to think, to enjoy, to love.

Marcus Aurelius

The greatest blessings of mankind are within us and within our reach. A wise man is content with his lot, whatever it may be, without wishing for what he has not.

Seneca

ABOUT THE AUTHOR

Born and raised in New Jersey, he spent 20 years living and working on Wall Street in New York City selling computer technology. He currently resides in Los Angeles and when he is not writing, he is involved in various facets of the logistics industry. He continues to apply the philosophy and teachings Freddie Clemett passed on to him throughout the course of their friendship. Christopher continues to write and search for the meaning of life. His books can be be discovered at www.ChristopherBlaire.com.

To reach Christopher or Freddie feel free to contact us at

Fridayswithfreddie@gmail.com

or at our website www.Fridayswithfredddie.com

COPYRIGHT

FIRST EDITION

Softcover ISBN: 978-1-7377286-5-8
Hardcover ISBN: 978-1-7377286-6-5
E-book ISBN: 978-1-7377286-4-1

Made in the USA
Las Vegas, NV
15 November 2023

80894330R00098